134 *Storm over Taos, New Mexico* (1930)
Courtesy Raymond and Raymond, Inc., New York

JOHN MARIN

Watercolors · Oil Paintings · Etchings

THE MUSEUM OF MODERN ART

REPRINT EDITION, 1966   PUBLISHED FOR
THE MUSEUM OF MODERN ART BY ARNO PRESS

Table of Contents

The exhibition has been selected from the following collections:

MR. A. E. GALLATIN, NEW YORK

MR. PHILIP GOODWIN, NEW YORK

MR. AND MRS. SAMUEL A. LEWISOHN, NEW YORK

MRS. EUGENE MEYER, WASHINGTON, D. C.

MISS GEORGIA O'KEEFFE, NEW YORK

MR. FAIRFIELD PORTER, NEW YORK

MR. PAUL ROSENFELD, NEW YORK

BRYNER-SCHWAB, NEW YORK

MR. ROBERT H. TANNAHILL, DETROIT, MICHIGAN

AN AMERICAN PLACE, NEW YORK

THE COLUMBUS GALLERY OF FINE ARTS, COLUMBUS, OHIO

FOGG ART MUSEUM, CAMBRIDGE, MASSACHUSETTS

THE METROPOLITAN MUSEUM OF ART, NEW YORK

PHILLIPS MEMORIAL GALLERY, WASHINGTON, D. C.

Portrait of John Marin by Gaston Lachaise (1927)

Preface and Acknowledgment

SAVE only the passage of relentless time, there is no severer test for a painter's work than a large retrospective exhibition. Paintings over a period of thirty or forty years, almost the whole of a man's life as an artist, are then exposed to the curious and critical public eye. Reputations carefully nurtured through a long series of discreetly limited exhibitions have sometimes been seriously deflated, or even blasted, by a retrospective of a hundred or more pictures. Too often then monotony and weakness are revealed rather than the richness and power of a master. Only a few men in every generation of artists can triumphantly endure such proving.

Is John Marin one of these? Not many American artists while they were still alive have had such extravagant admiration and so devout a following; and none perhaps has had such a persuasive advocate as Alfred Stieglitz. Indeed, though Mr. Stieglitz would not wish it said, this exhibition is in no small part a tribute to his devoted championship of Marin's work. Now, however, with his paintings hung on the neutral walls of the Museum, Marin must fight his own battle. Will he win? The writer, if he may be pardoned for taking sides in an official preface, believes positively that he will, and that the Museum's hospitality will be more than justified.

On behalf of the President and Trustees of the Museum the Director wishes to thank first of all Mr. Stieglitz who in spite of illness and the summer's heat has spent weeks of exacting work in selecting and preparing the paintings for exhibition; Miss Georgia O'Keeffe and Mr. William Einstein for their loyal assistance to Mr. Stieglitz; Mr. E. M. Benson, Marin's biographer, for his advice and help as

9

well as for his contribution to the catalog; Mr. Marsden Hartley, Marin's fellow artist, and Mr. Henry McBride, the art critic of the New York *Sun*, for their essays on Marin; Mr. Bernard Raymond, of Raymond and Raymond, Inc., for generously making possible the six color plates.

ALFRED H. BARR, JR., Director

John Marin

Of all those who have ever been professionally concerned or interested in the doings of John Marin I dare say I am his oldest acquaintance; and yet among all the gradually expanding group of those who pretend to know him, I also dare say I am the one who knows least of his personal idiosyncrasies. This is not so much carelessness on my part as a wilful preference—born in me the moment I began work as a critic of art—to form my estimate of a painting from the painting itself rather than from the manners of the artist at a dinner table. In fact I am not certain I ever saw John Marin eat, though I once did live for a short time in the same house with him, and this long years ago, befo' the war, and before any of Mr. Marin's numerous biographers had ever heard of him. It was in Venice, where Mr. Marin, with his step-mother, father, and brother descended upon the hotel I was domiciled in, and where I am certain I saw others of the family eat. But Mr. Marin was more furtive. You didn't see him do anything if he could help it. When cornered he was affability itself but if he saw you coming in time, or any of his family coming, he much preferred to bolt around the corner. Nevertheless I had several chats with him, the matter of which I have completely forgot. Probably we didn't discuss art, for at that time I had no more thought of becoming an art critic than he had of becoming America's premier aquarellist. But I liked him. There was no offense in his exclusiveness (or perhaps "apartness" is more descriptive). He was incorrigibly immersed in the business of interrogating nature for himself and had no time for interruptions. He conformed completely to my idea of an artist though I don't think I should have picked him out as one marked for worldly success. He already had the hatchet-hewn face that has since been made familiar to the world by Gaston Lachaise's portrait-bronze. Indeed I have never been able to see the slightest change in his lineaments made by the years and perturbations that have since rolled over our heads. He was born old and has remained young.

In Venice Mr. Marin was by way of being an etcher, and some of the prints achieved at that time still hold a place in the collections. Considerably later I heard of him in Paris as joining with a group of young American watercolourists sponsored by or attached to the American Club of those days. The little show the young men put on got into the cables, and probably because of that bit of luck, quickly came to America. When Marin shortly after appeared in the little gallery of Mr. Stieglitz at 291 Fifth Avenue, he already had so distinct a style in the use of watercolour that the work of the Parisian companions automatically faded from the scene. By this time I even forget who they were. But distinct as was the Marin style at the time of his first New York exhibitions there was nothing in it to disturb the sensibilities of purists. The colours were sparkling and pleasant and practically every drawing could be called honestly a poem. It was a young man's irresistible lyricism that impelled them. They were not profound but they were natural and unforced.

There was much commendation for them, particularly upon the lips of young people. I recall no adverse criticisms. Possibly the water-colours were not sufficiently challenging to upset official opinion; but the younger connoisseurs do not look for profundities from their own set but for assurance. The one among them who doesn't ask how it should be done but goes ahead and does it, gets their admiration at once. Marin, for all of his "apartness" seemed to respond to this approbation just like a regular human being and with each show he put on, his assurance gained and very soon he painted with an authority that at times was positively militant. When the young people told Marin he was "great," apparently he felt he had to be great. There was also the obligation to justify "291." In the little gallery generalled by Mr. Stieglitz so much pulling down of the Academy had been done that suddenly it dawned upon all the talkers and lis-

60 *Headed for Boston* (1923)
Courtesy Raymond and Raymond, Inc., New York

teners that some building up had to be done, too. Marin, of course, was occasionally among the listeners and though no fingers were pointed directly at him his subconscious got on the job and produced results. The light-hearted singing troubadour who had come from Paris changed into a serious dramatist almost over night. The little dancing boats in the harbour from which the artist had previously heard tinkling melodies now bounced about on positively black waves and against gray skies; and the recurring tune sounded mighty like a dirge. The towering buildings of lower New York also occupied his attention and he did them in a perfect frenzy of appreciation of their significance and importance. He became an excited and exciting painter. The war by this time had come upon us and had a lot to do with this nervousness of Marin. In personal contacts he seemed as cool and aloof as Voltaire is said to have been during the Seven Years War but when the year's supply of watercolours was collected by Mr. Stieglitz for his annual Marin show, it was noticed that the passion in the drawings amounted to violence. Fortunately they were practically abstract and as the numbers of persons at that time in America capable of apprehending an artist's emotion when expressed in abstract terms was limited, no unnecessary increase in the current war fury could be traced to them. The drawings themselves, however, were certainly furious but I think it was merely Marin's response to the furiousness that was in the air. In any case there is an explosiveness about the "downtown series" of drawings and about a group of sunset pictures of the same period that sets them apart from the entire range of Marin's work and gives them an especial interest. Dynamics are not necessarily a value in themselves but a pure expression reinforced by unusual energy naturally takes precedence over milder statements from the same source. There is such a thing, of course, as tearing a passion to tatters, of applying too much power to too frail a theme, as poor Caruso did in his last two breathless years with the "furtiva lagrima" that had previously been so exquisite; but Marin was fortunate in his rages to be raging against such things as Maine sunsets

13

and New York skyscrapers; subjects, one must admit, that can stand any amount of pressure.

After the war, Marin calmed down much in advance of the rest of the populace, and his mountain views in New Mexico and his accounts of ships in distress off the coast of New England had a precision of statement that suggested a serene mind. There was still a certain amount of excitement in them, for Marin is an artist who catches fire from a motif, but it is a contained excitement like that in Gluck's Orfeo and vehemence was not allowed to interfere with elegance. As elegance seems to be more in request than passion, it happens that Marin's later days have witnessed an increase in his public, and so it is not so strange to have an extended representation of his work in a public museum as it would have seemed once. Elegance, however, cannot have been a conscious pursuit of his, and it may occasion him some surprise to be told that he has it, for elegance, like style itself, is, or ought to be, unaware. . . . It's just the bloom on the peach—but it's what sells the peach.

HENRY McBRIDE

As to John Marin, and his ideas

A<small>ROUND</small> Nineteen hundred and nine, I met with a certain picture in water colour of a scene in Piccadilly, London—which was of course, of a bus and all that gathers around it, and this water colour impressed me as different because it was not sweet and dainty, and later, on the outer edge of this rectangle, I saw a curious man who might have been the joker at the grave of Yorick, and somehow I sort of see this same image as I look at him now, because there is always a play of earthy humour about to fall like an autumn leaf from his face, and in and out of the diameter and circumference of these memories they pass like wondrous wraiths of living fire because they were all so alive then, and those that come to my mind as I speak are living somewhere else, and so we do not come upon them any more in the old living ways.

The living place was of course "291" because it was at the end of the run or the walk on Fifth Avenue, diagonally across from the Holland House, one of the then nicest hotels in New York, where Joe the waiter would say the right thing to everyone and see they got what they wanted in the way they wanted, and would talk about the figures on stock exchange tapes, and was getting tips from his wealthy patrons, and no doubt giving a few.

There was a round table there for lunch every day and one saw many different and possibly grotesque looking men there because they plowed their way across the street on the invitation of Alfred Stieglitz, in and out of hansoms, or perhaps letting pass the Vanderbilt coach with its double or was it triple span of horses, with a Vanderbilt on the box, and you heard the clicking of white reins over the spick horses' backs, and the crack of the whip would be heard for blocks.

It was then that the young Ethel Barrymore was making a hit of it in "Captain Jinks," and her smart uncle John Drew was arranging his profile, because a defect in one eye had taught him how to conceal this and of which he made a really fine art.

Caruso would be found on the avenue with his bacchanalian bulk, his sensuous eyes and his very tender and human smile, for he was notoriously kind, there was Mark Twain always in white, and I remember so well at the very last he was dressed in white and covered with violets, and there was Mrs. Philip Lydig to startle with her amazing silhouettes, and it was all just like that.

There were some smallish pastels about the edges of the room at "291" and they were a bit whistlerish, and yet they were not whistlerish, but this water colour of Piccadilly made me feel then like saying if this man is not careful he will turn out to be a different water colour painter, he will have very different ideas about this medium, for they were done in a decidedly escapist style, that is to say, they were handled in a way this medium had not been handled before, for they were upsetting the notion first that Winslow Homer had said the first and last word, taken this medium out of the hands of the meticulous and finicky ones, for remember it was once given over to ladies in finishing schools, then it got to be the relief medium of tied up bachelors, then it got into the hands of men like Winslow Homer and the Maris brothers, and see what a change has come over it through the iconoclastic efforts of John Marin, once of Rutherford, New Jersey.

It is twenty-five years since the Piccadilly London bus water colour and you will find this very picture out of the private collection of Alfred Stieglitz in this present retrospective exhibition of the Museum of Modern Art, and you will find something you never saw before, you will find that Marin has lifted water colour painting out of the embroidery class, out of the class of minor accomplishments of the idle ladies and fussy bachelors—what's that you are saying, one hears even now among the intelligent, and has made of it a major medium.

The Sung painters have done hundreds of scrolls that reveal the historical tremolo of leaves in the wind, of fog flying over conic

16

mountains, and if you are careful in your observations you will find a lot of that same sense of surety of observation, and of surety of brush stroke in this conspicuous American, and Marin has given this ancient sense of surety a thousand times all over his water colours, but he has been wise enough never to disturb the surface of the paper which is I feel the chief crime of Winslow Homer, torn up the paper to get a seemingly heavier body tone, the which has always failed because it goes below the surface and the surface is where the picture belongs.

Perhaps Cubism has been a sort of hilarious influence at times in these water colours and the natural wit of Marin has cooperated in ways that make us wonder why, but for all that, don't be bothered, but just let these pictorial beauties settle in your eye, and you will find something like treasures from the Kimberly mines in them, which after they have been lapidated by the intelligence leave you with first rate gems the like of which you have not encountered before.

No one has known better what the prescribed wash can do, no one has made it more powerful, more velvety, more metallic, more acrid or more sinister and more provocative of the great sources of nature and especially the sea and the shores that bound it, alas my native land of Maine which I am always being told about by one good painter, this being Marin, and a lot of bad painters, but Marin gets those still, esoteric stretches where islands float in other world ethers, and gives them the look of prearranged mirages.

No one has so completely realized in this medium the exact condition of a high moment better than this man, and for myself, and mind you I speak for myself only, many a time Marin has saved my life in the past because he has brought esoteric release to me by some of those strangest and completely revealing washes that have ever been done by anyone, and you must care for the wash first of all in this medium for there is nothing else to recommend it.

Take in a few Turners, all so thin and pale and if perhaps slightly evocative, never having that brute arm of thought behind them to make them into vital issues, follow the line of development by way of the Maris brothers, then to Sargeant, Homer, John Whorf, Eliot O'Hara and the lessers and you will find that Marin pulls in the race because he has literally done more with the same sort of limitations, and he cannot ever be legitimately accused of being fussy and fumbling, which is not to be denied of most or all the others, and you never find that sense of universal scope in them as you do in Marin, either.

I am not rooting for Marin, I am just saying he has done all there is to be done with this medium, and let anyone else try to re-invent it if he can, and he will be a welcome addition. First of all Marin has loved his medium, his work, and his life. He has spent six and a half decades telling the world that the privileges of beauty are enormous, that it even affects those that have no experience of it, though he has concentrated on the first five words because they are true statement and all the others in the statement are conjecture.

You will never see water colours like these of John Marin again so take a good look and remember, and if you are a painter, don't try to cope with the style because the style in this case is several times the man, love of life, love of work, love of nature, and the love of the enormous privilege.

If you consult the work of John Marin you will see that he paces his strokes to a new beat though it is the same language, just as in the world of poetry T. S. Eliot has plussed all the forms by the dynamic approach of his own, and so Marin is isolated from all others even in spite of himself for Marin is not a smart aleck, he is keen as a whip, alert as a razor, and has the grip of steel on his medium, and find that anywhere else in the whole range of water colour painting if you can, and even when he is casual he is still more alive than any one. Strength is always a personal thing and this is the case of the mighty Marin.

If you are a live wire yourself you will feel different after a gulp of Marin water colours, if not—you will be like the others—simply apathetic, and isn't this the meaning of any really good painting, to feel different after it, somehow different?

MARSDEN HARTLEY

18

John Marin
—"and pertaining thereto"

"People can think what they wish about my art,
but this much I know, it is really mine."

CONSTABLE

JOHN MARIN is an isolated figure in contemporary American art. He has never identified himself with any school or doctrine of painting either domestic or foreign. He has few followers and no disciples. For twenty-seven years he has exhibited his work at the various galleries[1] over which Alfred Stieglitz has faithfully presided. Today at the age of sixty-six he is as uncompromising a free-lance as he was at thirty-six. A lyricist by endowment, his art is an expression of his love for nature's forms. Perhaps no American artist—I can think of no exceptions—has courted Nature more tirelessly and with greater understanding of all her seasonal moods.

Boats and buildings are as much his province as skies, seas, islands, and mountains. He has stamped his creative signature on all of them —a signature which many of us have come to regard as unique in American art. This, it seems to me, is abundantly confirmed by the current exhibition at the Museum of Modern Art. Here you will find the golden harvest of a lifetime: the joyous record of countless struggles to remake nature after her own image.

It is significant, I think, that among all the works included in the present show you will not find a single still-life, a Reclining Nude, a Portrait of My Wife—or any of the traditional stock-in-trade subject matter of the studio artist. We can safely assume that Marin hasn't a remnant of the stay-at-home genre painter in his make-up. His interests are completely external to the atmosphere of his home or his

[1] "291," or The Photo-Secession Gallery, the Intimate Gallery, and An American Place.

work-shop. He has what amounts to a physical abhorrence of any form of artificial posturing whether it is a hired model or a studied assemblage of still-life objects. "Nature's arrangements," Marin wrote to Stieglitz in 1914, during his first summer at West Point, Maine, "are finer, more, infinitely finer than your studio arrangements, my fine studio arrangements. Chap, just try and arrange some chairs in a room. Does the room look homey? . . . But that doesn't mean," he hastens to add, "that on your canvas you cannot use these great natural foundlings and juggle and mould and play to your heart's content."

A whimsical and not very cogent utterance, to be sure, but one that casts a sharp light on the creative personality of its author. The truth of the matter is that studio arrangements, chairs, and even the people who sit in them, have always meant considerably less to Marin than nature's playground, the great outdoors. "Seems to me," Marin has said, "that the true artist must perforce go from time to time to the elemental big forms — Sky, Sea, Mountain, Plain — and those things pertaining thereto, to sort of re-true himself up, to recharge the battery. For these big forms have everything. But to express these, you have to love these, to be a part of these in sympathy. One doesn't get very far without this love, this love to enfold too the relatively little things that grow on the mountain's back. Which if you don't recognize, you don't recognize the mountain."[1]

And yet Marin is by no means to be regarded as a romantic artist in the sense that Homer Martin, Inness, Blakelock, and the Hudson River painters were romantic, or the adherents of the Barbizon school, or their German contemporaries, Caspar David Friedrich and Arnold Böcklin. Unlike these artists Marin brings no twilight moods of revery, allegory, or pastoral pantheism to his art. Nor does he attempt to convert literary or philosophic ideas into visual terms. Marin's romanticism is cut from another cloth—the cloth from which Claude Lorrain, Dürer, Cézanne, and Winslow Homer fashioned their

[1] From "Marin on Himself," published in *Creative Art*, October, 1928.

20

watercolors. It is the romance of detachment from the harsh economics of survival: the ability to observe a tree, a boat, a wave, a sand-dune, a grain elevator, or a skyscraper as though all life's noblest music were enclosed in their straining forms. He does this without the subjective anthropomorphism of the expressionist, or the factual fanaticism of the naturalist. He sees and feels these forms as purposive organic elements and seeks to recreate them in plastic symbols that are strictly germane to the medium employed—whether this happens to be the drawn line, the print, the watercolor, or the oil painting.

How successful Marin has been we now have ample opportunity to judge. It seems to me that even his "failures" are scarcely less stimulating than his successes. The reason for this is that for Marin each new work is the product of a completely fresh encounter with subject matter. So that even though the work itself may not be perfectly realized, it generally succeeds in communicating the full sensuous impact of the artist's experience. Whereas the failure of a more intellectual craftsman is often a meaningless *pastiche*, Marin's failures retain an indestructible core of original perception that can be enjoyed despite its formal imperfections. It is this need for constant replenishment from the subsoil of inspired experience that prevents Marin from ever becoming more concerned with the method than the content of expression. It has also served to protect him from the quicksand of speculation for its own sake, and from falling headlong into the arms of the many attractive "Isms" that have punctuated the history of contemporary art. At most he was a "fellow-traveller," and then only during the early experimental phases of his work.

Temperamentally incapable of "being moved" to creation by anything foreign to the substance of his own vision, Marin did not, however, remain wholly untouched by the torrents of aesthetic theory and practice that fell like shrapnel from the climactic skies of the times. In his earliest drawings—several of which are exhibited—made years before he attended an art school, during leisurely sketching trips down the Delaware River and as far west as the Mississippi Basin, Marin already clearly indicated an Impressionist's preoccupation with "filtering light." "The most important person in any picture," he might then have agreed with Manet, "is the light." It was not from this founder of *Plein-airism* that the torch of Impressionism was passed on to Marin, but from James McNeill Whistler, the American-born playboy of Impressionism, and the leading mouthpiece of that isolationist creed, Art for Art's Sake.

Impressionism was less a scientific theory for Marin than a point of view with which he was vaguely in accord—as much so as a person trained to be an architect, and who actually practiced this profession for four or five years, could be. It was this factual training that groomed him for the healthy precepts of Thomas P. Anshutz, a pupil of Thomas Eakins, and one of Marin's instructors at the Pennsylvania Academy of the Fine Arts. Under Anshutz's tutelage Marin broadened his observation by adding to his inherent interest in landscape and buildings, an interest in the human form. An Eakins-Rembrandtian quality enters Marin's work of this period. We find him combing the city and suburbs of Philadelphia for subjects suitable to his pen: men sitting on benches in Independence Square; tall, tightly bodiced women with the braided coiffure of the period leaning listlessly against window casements, or sewing by lamplight; sailboats at anchor in the ship-canal; cars on railroad sidings discharging their freight. For these drawings Marin won a prize in 1900. Between 1901 and 1903 we find him at the Art Students' League in New York testing his wings for future flight, and in 1905 on a ship bound for Europe.

Here was no fledgling embarking with romantic enthusiasm on his *Wanderjahr* under foreign skies. Marin, one should remember, had already thirty-five years behind him; had been hard at work for some fifteen of them; and had a mature conception of what he wanted to be and do. Whistler, for the moment, was his pole star. With Paris as his headquarters Marin set out to retrace the steps of the dead master

117 *On Morse Mountain, Small Point, Maine* (1928)
Courtesy Raymond and Raymond, Inc., New York

(he died in 1903). He went to Amsterdam, Venice, London, and then, growing weary of playing follow the leader, he began ploughing a path of his own. But while he was under the Whistlerian spell he made many fine etchings which, though obviously in the spirit of "the sublime coxcomb," were no mere imitative transcriptions but the inspired shorthand of an original talent.

To Whistler's superbly delicate generalizations Marin brought a genius for documenting particulars (*cf.*, his etching *L'Opéra, Paris,* of 1908, plate no. 73 in check-list of etchings; one should never forget that he was an architect before he was an artist) and a sense of space which is far more dramatic than Whistler's. It was not only the Debussyan nuance that Marin was after but the precise linear statement as well as the sharp discord. Technically Marin has remained Whistler's inferior as an etcher, but at his best he is always his equal, and occasionally his superior. Such plates as *Bridge Canal, Amsterdam,* of 1906 (plate no. 9 in check-list of etchings), *Ponte Ghetto, Venice,* of 1907 (plate no. 49 in check-list of etchings), *L'Opéra, Paris,* of 1908, *The Cathedral near the Old Market, Rouen,* of 1909 (plate no. 91 in check-list of etchings), and *Chartres Cathedral* of 1910 (plate no. 96 in check-list of etchings)—to choose only a few of his early etchings—place Marin in the ranks of the foremost printmakers. However, these etchings were still distinctly nineteenth century in flavor. When one calls to mind the work which the rebellious *Fauves* and Cubists were doing during this period, Marin's etchings, fine as they are, can hardly be said to be in the spirit of the age. Marin was still fascinated by the picturesque. Not the "pretty picture," to be sure, honeyed with Pre-Raphaelite sentimentality, but the romantic vista, the "quaint" thoroughfare, courtyard, or building, the cathedral façade, etc. It was his choice of subject more than his treatment of it that marked him as a child of the nineteenth century.

That Marin could have been unaware of the many art movements which were exploding like giant firecrackers under his very nose seems hardly credible—and certainly it is no feather in his cap—but, as far as I have been able to determine, it is none the less true. It was not until his final return to America in 1911 (he returned on a short visit in 1909) that he received his first real introduction to the art of Cézanne, Picasso, Matisse, *le Douanier* Rousseau, Picabia, Brancusi, and other avantgardists, at Alfred Stieglitz's Photo-Secession Gallery in New York. In Paris their existence was comparatively unknown to him, though I have good reason to believe that he knew and admired the work of Monet, Degas, and particularly Toulouse-Lautrec and Constantin Guys. Like most young artists of the time Marin was enamored of the Japanese, Hokusai, Hiroshige, and Utamaro.

Among the "old masters" of the western world Marin had few loves. He has since learnt to cast an appreciative eye on Tintoretto, El Greco, Rubens, van Eyck, Constable, and van Gogh, as well as on several of his contemporaries, but I doubt whether these artists spoke a clear or persuasive language to him in Paris. Unlike Cézanne, Marin did not haunt the Louvre, and had no desire to "make of Impressionism something solid and enduring, like the art of the museums." There was nothing of the art scholar in him. Museums he found, did more to confuse than to enlighten him, and, for the most part, he steered his course by another star. His likes, as I have tried to indicate, were based exclusively on that variable emulsion, that chameleon quantity known as kinship. And he was and is incapable of being even superficially interested in any art or aesthetic problem alien to his deepest feelings and *modus operandi*. This insular cast of mind is a serious limitation as well as a rare virtue, and I do not know whether the loss in Marin's case is greater than the gain. I do know that his art thrived on it, and who is to say what an artist's intellectual and cultural diet should be as long as his art continues to flourish.

And flourish it did in all fields but one, namely that of oil painting. During the years of Marin's residence abroad he printed the bulk of his etchings (99 of a total of 132) and was no less busily engaged at watercolor and oil painting, mediums in which he had won local

24

distinction quite early in his career and which have since become his major preoccupations. In 1908 the Luxembourg Museum, for reasons only known to its directorate, purchased one of Marin's oils, *The Mills of Meaux*, painted in 1906. I have only seen a photograph of this picture and cannot pass judgment on its paint quality. But in the black and white form in which I know it it does not appear to be a work of any considerable distinction. Though ably and compactly designed, the method, if not the inspiration, seems to be that of Monet and his Impressionist colleagues. Little more can be said for the other oils of this period which I *have* seen. Paradoxically the most fragmentary of them—and from the public's point of view the least successful—show the greatest promise.[1] At best they contain the forthright but fragile poetry of a novitiate who felt the restraining shackles of the painting tradition and was powerless at the time to free himself. It was not until some twenty years later, when Marin had already made a formidable contribution as a watercolorist, that he again tackled the oil painting hobgoblins of his youth, and vanquished many of them.

In watercolor the voice of tradition seemed less dictatorial to Marin. Its academic priesthood had as yet formulated no rigid Pentateuch of procedure. It was a game for which each player was free to make his own rules, providing, of course, that these rules did not conflict with the unwritten formal laws of the medium. It was more intimate and more personal than oil painting, but no less exacting. And, all things considered, it was, at the time, more suitable to Marin's volatile temperament. Marin had been working in watercolor since 1888, but it was not until 1908 that he hit his stride. *London Omnibus* of this year (plate no. 1) was one of the first pieces of pure ore which Marin drew up from the rich deposits of his genius. Although sired by Impressionism, his method had already passed from an atmospheric to an architectonic stage. Marin had built with

[1] *Cf.*, reproduction facing page 20 of *John Marin: The Man and His Work*, by E. M. Benson, The American Federation of Arts, 1935.

solid blocks of pure color toward a structural climax in which all its parts seem joined in a tight yet fluid circuit of rhythmic movement; a small but perfect statement made with a sure hand and a light heart. It was Seurat humanized, made more supple and more responsive to the changing pulse of visual appearance. A twentieth century artist emerged from this watercolor: an artist who looked at the world through eyes adjusted to the focus of new facts.

Marin henceforth threw orthodox procedure overboard and let his best instincts be his guide. For he felt that they could now be trusted to take him safely to his port of call. In his Seine watercolors of 1908 and 1909 he gave a cohesive character to each of his works by respecting the dominant accent of the sky and the insistence with which its mood is mirrored in everything else: *A Rolling Sky*, 1908, wraps the earth in a single rhythm; a spotted sky (*cf., Four O'Clock on the Seine*, plate no. 5) casts its reflection on the broken, nervous pattern of the bridge and river; a soft, lightly overcast sky (*cf. Along the Seine*) deepens the velvet handwriting of boats gliding in the blue wash of the Seine, and is again echoed in the slow curves of the bridge-arches crossing it.

From these Seine watercolors Marin turned with equal understanding to the human form in his *Girl Sewing* of 1910 (plate no. 9) and to the mountain and tree forms of his Tyrolean series of the same year. Marin had again broken fresh ground in these pictures. It was the first time he had used such subjects as leading, rather than incidental, themes. The *Girl Sewing* has a human tenderness which we rarely find in Marin's work. Of the Tyrol group, *Tyrol at Kufstein* (plate no. 11) is perhaps the consummate accomplishment. It is to the Seine watercolors and the *Girl Sewing* what orchestral music is to chamber music. It is the first-born of a monumental family of mountain pictures which includes *The Sun of Suffern* of 1925 (plate no. 68), a simmering sun hanging over a shaggy bulwark of palisade; *Mt. Chocorua* of 1926, baring its bounteous bosom to a windswept sky; *White Mountains, Autumn* of 1927 (plate no. 99) with its rich

26

143 *Phippsburg, Maine* (1932)
Courtesy Raymond and Raymond, Inc., New York

carpet of foliage, its clusters of scrub pine outlined against black layers of mountain; *Franconia Range* of the same year, an undulating panorama of cleft and pointed peaks; and, finally, the patriarch of them all, *Storm Over Taos* of 1930 (frontispiece), the epic of the big form and the small form united in a flawless chorus of color and line.

Marin's long period of expatriation ended in 1911. He had drunk liberally of the old world, and its flavor was still on his lips. He now found himself elbowing his way through the Babylon that was America in the pre-jazz age. The Palisades looked surprisingly good to him. So did the Hudson River with its puffing cargo. And the Brooklyn Bridge, glistening like a necklace of burnished silver in the dust-saturated sunlight. And Downtown, New York, with its milling masses and mushroom litter of skyscrapers. There was no sense of order here but only raw power determined to go places: the dynamite of growth through speculation. Marin felt "like a drunkard skating on ice."[1] He was both fascinated and frightened, like a child by a stroke of lightning. It was not social causes that he saw but aesthetic effects, the abstract effects of color and line, of mass and movement competing for a place in the sun.

"I have just started some Downtown stuff," wrote Marin to Stieglitz in 1911, "and to pile these great houses one upon another with paint as they do pile themselves up there so beautiful, so fantastic—at times one is afraid to look at them but feels like running away." However, he did not run away. He stood his ground and tried to take stock of his explosive environment in watercolors and etchings of a quickened pulse. Swift slashing lines of color, veins filled with the mercury of tension and strain which define the thrust of upward movements of mass, or flying buttresses of sky forms; the electric staccato of dots which are endless rows of windows; the splash of molten color or vibrating waves of line which simulate the sun. This molecular war of the physical elements was waged on the bat-

[1] With apologies to Maxim Gorky who coined this phrase. He used it in a commemorative article on Anton Chekov to describe the pathetic efforts of a pedagogue to impress his listeners.

tlefield of Marin's art. How successfully, we can see by examining his "famous" Woolworth watercolors of 1912 and 1913,[1] as well as his etching series of the same subject. "I see great forces at work," wrote Marin at the time of the great Armory Show, "great movements; the large buildings and the small buildings; the warring of the great and the small; influences of one mass on another greater or smaller mass . . . each subject in some degree to the other's power. . . . I can hear the sound of their strife," Marin concluded, "and there is great music being played." Music such as no American had heard and recorded since the dawn of the twentieth century.

Technically this repercussive period of Marin's work was immensely instructive to him. It taught him the value of the stenographic phrase, and, what was still more important, of so adjusting the dynamic forms within his picture that they achieved a "blessed equilibrium" within their borders without any need for the artifice of a frame. In subduing the fighting forces of his art Marin's enclosure forms were evolved; those embracing accents of design which are already noticeable in his earliest work (*viz:* the canal coping, bridge, and water reflections forming a closed pattern in his etching, *Bridge Canal, Amsterdam* of 1906, plate no. 9 in check-list) and are soon to appear as mature elements of picture-construction (*cf., Maine Islands* of 1922, plate no. 50, and *Two-master Becalmed* of 1923, plate no. 53). They are never arbitrary stylistic devices pressed into service, but are structurally inherent in the subject matter and develop from it. They are nature's accents reinterpreted on a formal plane. They also serve the purpose of directing the observer's gaze along sequential channels of related movement. They are, in short, the artist's instruments of orchestration to be used as his experience, training, and vision dictate.[2]

Although lower Manhattan has always remained a permanent part

[1] First exhibited in the Armory Show of 1913. Five of these watercolors, from the collection of Mrs. Eugene Meyer, are included in the present exhibition, nos. 13-17. See plate no. 15.

[2] *Cf.*, Benson, *op. cit.*, pages 31-32, 66, 79-83, for a more thorough discussion of the origin, use, and development of Marin's "enclosure forms."

of Marin's diet, it has by no means been the whole of it. There is at bottom an anti-big-city sediment in Marin: an instinctive resentment against this Xanthippe whose shrill voice often drowns out her finer qualities. And yet, it is not that he loves the city less, but that he loves the country more. The Berkshires, the Adirondacks, the coast of Maine, the Delaware River country of Pennsylvania, the White Mountains, New Mexico—here Marin spent the better part of a lifetime of summers among pines that rise like pyramids or bend to the rough embrace of the wind; among lakes that lick their shores in receding ripples, and mountains that leap like trout from a green basin of meadow; among fast-moving tides, rocks blistered with barnacles, dromedary sand dunes, ships without number, seas that drink the palette of the sky, and villages of white houses clinging to the edge of the sea or cradled among tall elms; among the slag of New Mexico's volcanic mountains, its dry sage grass, its streams that run earth-red under the dazzling Klieg lights of a desert sun. Here on the hot anvil of nature's furnace Marin forged the art we know him by, an art as protean as the sources of its inspiration.

The Maine coast, more than any other single locale, was the nursery and testing-ground of Marin's art. Here especially he went to school with his environment, drawing wisdom from the waves, the surf-washed stones and shells sparkling in the pockets of the sand (*cf., The Little Boat*, 1914, plate no. 19); from the shapes of trees and shrubbery crystalline in the prismatic sunlight (*cf., Rock and Scrub Pine, Small Point, Maine*, 1916, plate no. 29; *Tree and Sea, Maine*, 1919, plate no. 32; and *Sunset, Casco Bay*, 1919, plate no. 35), or pressed into a flat pattern of geometric design (*cf., Spruce with Moss, Small Point, Maine*, 1914; *Tree Forms, Stonington*, 1919); from the condensed aspect of a broad vista of shore, sea, islands, ships, and buildings caught in the net of a single mood (*cf., Maine Islands*, 1922, plate no. 50, *Stonington, Maine*, 1923, plate no. 62); the warm texture of near objects and the cool quality of distant ones; the sharp contrast of the rough and the smooth;

the abrupt leap from yellow to blue and the smoother passage from yellow to green or red.

This knowledge, like all knowledge, was not secured without its price of perspiration and heartache. It was a slow and painful process of accretion rather than, as the layman imagines, a series of apocalyptic revelations. Conceived of pleasure, Marin's art was, nevertheless, born of pain. His job was made doubly difficult by reason of the iron fidelity with which he held himself answerable not only to the unwritten laws of his medium but to the full flavor of his experience in nature. It was one thing to produce a work of high technical excellence—another to make it a truly organic equivalent for its inspirational source. "However abstractly, however symbolically expressed," wrote Marin of his work in contrast with the "European eyed abstractions" of those Americans whose art is "a monumental memory of other things,"— "I would still have it, 'Town of Stonington,' 'The boats of Maine,' 'The people of Maine,' 'The sheep of the Maine isles,' seething with the whole atmosphere of Maine. . . . Let's try now to illustrate a point. This is the prow of a ship. I draw abstractly. It's cut up, yet not cut up. It does things, it assumes directions and leanings yet is not really cut up. In all its movements it remains a whole. It doesn't lose track. Mr. Fisherman, he doesn't maybe understand, yet he's made to feel something like he feels as he knows the prows of ships." [1]

This passionate struggle to remain faithful to the character of his subject is constantly echoed in the specific titles which he gives to his pictures: *Becalmed; Before the Wind; Sun Spots; Deep-sea Trawlers; Tide Riff, Mouth of Kennebeck; Speed, Lake Champlain.* It is not just any place, but Parker Head, Morse Mountain, Blue Mountains on the Circle Drive near Taos, Looking up Fifth Avenue from Thirtieth Street. Not just any boat but a two-master, three-master, four-master, fishing smack, schooner. Not just any sea but blue sea, grey sea. Not just any season of the year but spring, summer,

[1]From a letter to Alfred Stieglitz dated October 1919, Stonington, Maine.

autumn, winter. At the core of Marin's broadest generalizations one usually discovers the fertile sperm of organic truth.

Were it possible to trace the successive steps of Marin's technical development we should probably find that they are all closely related to some insistent aspect of his physical environment. These steps can be roughly summarized as follows:

1) The widening of Marin's watercolor palette from primary washes of cerulean, cobalt, or ultramarine blue with only secondary accents of yellow (aureolin, yellow ochre, cadmium), red (rose madder, light red, spectrum red), green (viridian, oxide of chromium), and Payne's grey to their countervalent use in which all but yellow play equally important rôles and to which a lustrous black is later added and a more frequent use made of pencilled notations either under or over washes of color.

2) The broad, condensed "and pertaining thereto" vista whose movements extend into the picture depth but are invariably brought forward to the frontal plane by means of sky forms or some other integrative element of functional design (cf., *Marin Island*, 1915, plate no. 26; *Lower Manhattan from the River, No. 2*, 1921, plate no. 39; *Pertaining to Stonington Harbor, Maine*, 1926, plate no. 78; *Pertaining to Deer Isle—the Harbor. Deer Isle, Maine Series, No. 1*, 1927, plate no. 84).

3) The use within a single picture of several compartmental episodes or closed sections, each a separate yet related unit of construction, like the phrases in a musical score[1] (cf., among the watercolors: *Telephone Building*, 1926; *Phippsburg, Maine*, 1932, illustrated opposite page 26; among the etchings: *Downtown, New York*, 1924; *River Movement*, 1925, plate no. 125 in check-list of etchings; among the oils: *Women Forms and Sea*, 1934, plate no. 177; *Composition No. 2 Cape Split, Maine*, 1933).

[1] What the enclosure forms are to the total orchestration of the picture the compartmental episodes are to its parts. They were first introduced in 1921-1923 and by 1926 their more rigid diagrammatic use was abandoned.

The most important single factor to influence the course of Marin's development since 1925 was his return to oil painting, a medium which he never completely abandoned, though he pursued it less diligently than watercolor or etching. This reawakening of interest in oil painting had its origin mainly in the fact that since 1919 Marin had been doing an increasing amount of work in his studio rather than directly before nature. "I find that now working out of doors tires me," he wrote to Stieglitz in the fall of 1919. "I don't get what I want any more and seem to think I can do better visualizing what I have experienced through my eyes." As a result he became gradually less dependent on the immediate external stimulus and more concerned with the architectonic anatomy of his art. This was first apparent in the watercolor series of New York waterfront and street-scene subjects that were done during 1920 and 1921 (*cf.*, *Lower Manhattan*, 1920, *Singer Building*, 1921, *Lower Manhattan*, 1921[1]) and even more so in his late work with the same and other subject matter (*cf.*, *The Black Sun*, 1926, illustrated opposite page 16; *Street Crossing*, 1928, plate no. 100; *Broadway, Night*, plate no. 119; *New York from the West Shore Ferry*; and *Dance of the San Domingo Indians*, plate no. 126—all of 1929).

Working habits are not easily altered, and when Marin took up his oil palette again he found himself using its pigments as thinly as though they were a fluid aqueous medium. (The final phase of Cézanne's painting in oil seems to have been similarly influenced by his work in watercolor; but whereas in Cézanne's case this method of using oil was both purposeful and profoundly successful, in Marin's it was a less purposeful and less meaningful transference of working habits from one medium to another.) His colors were narrowly limited in harmonic and mechanical relationships and were distributed in areas of flat decorative pattern that had the appearance—as indeed it was—of an experimental exercise. There are, to my knowledge,

[1] *Cf.*, reproduction facing page 52 of Benson, *op. cit.* This picture was reproduced in color in the *Dial* portfolio.

178 *Circus Forms* (1934)
Courtesy Raymond and Raymond, Inc., New York

only two felicitous exceptions to the above: *Related to Brooklyn Bridge, New York*, and *Related to St. Paul's, New York*, of 1928, both of which are in a class with Marin's most successful city subjects and are among his finest oils, albeit they are more loosely and decoratively knit than most.

In contrast with the swiftness of watercolor execution, the new discipline of working on an oil in shifts over a long period, must have fallen "like cold chains" upon this Ishmaelite who "never sat with his wings furled for six months together."

Marin's oils of 1929 to 1932 consist principally of seascapes loaded with hot color (*cf., Rocks and Sea, Small Point, Maine*, 1931, plate. no. 162) done during long summers at Maine and shorter visits to Lake Champlain and Jones Beach; and of New York street scenes painted with equally thick pigments but a narrower color palette (*cf., Mid-Manhattan, I*, 1932) during winters at Cliffside, New Jersey. While the former group is richer in color and more vigorously painted, the latter contains the instrumental music of a more controled art.

The period from 1933 to the present divides itself into exactly the same categories of subject matter except that the scales now shift still further from outdoor to indoor studio painting, and the human form is finally introduced on a large scale—repercussions of which are to be found in Marin's recent watercolors (*cf., Young Man of the Sea*, 1934, plate no. 159). The high spots of this period in oil are reached in (1) *Pertaining to Fifth Avenue and Forty-Second Street* of 1933 (plate no. 171), with its interlocking forms à la Tintoretto and its low-keyed color harmonies; (2) *Composition No. 2, Cape Split, Maine* of the same year, one of the most complex problems of design ever tackled by Marin and admirably resolved; (3) *Circus Forms* of 1934 (illustrated opposite page 32), which despite a certain naiveté in conception I consider Marin's most witty and delightful oil both in color and design; (4) *From Seeing Cape Split, Maine*, of 1935 (plate no. 180) which has all the warmth and accuracy of touch of Marin's finest watercolors, yet attained by strictly oil painting means.

It appears that Marin secures his best results in oil when he is least hampered by problematic considerations, when he depends on the strength of his feelings to carry him over the rough seas of his subject. Whether he will ever succeed in making his oils speak the Promethean language of his watercolors is a moot question, and I prefer, for the moment, to let it rest in the broad lap of Time. On no other score do Marin's achievements deserve an indecisive judgment. He has carried the art of watercolor to a height seldom equaled in American art or the art of our time. He has broken many aesthetic commandments held sacred by the watchdogs of culture only to create others more in keeping with the spirit of his age. I believe with Marin that essentially his pictures "are conservative and belong to convention." Not the whalebone dogma of the academy or the salon but the larger life-giving conventions to which the artist-pioneers of all ages have added their own Reformations.

E. M. BENSON

Biographical Information

1870-1899

John Marin was born in Rutherford, N. J., December 23, 1870. Grandfather on father's side came from Paris. Grandparents on mother's side lived in Peekskill before the Revolution and New Brunswick after it. They were Loyalists. His mother, Annie Louise Currey, died when he was nine days old. He was raised by grandmother Currey and two aunts at Weehawken, N. J., where he lived until his twenty-sixth year. Attended public school in Union Hill (two or three years), Hoboken Academy (two years), Stevens Preparatory (four years), and Stevens Institute (one year). Held odd jobs, one with notion-goods house, for about two years. Four years in architects' offices. Free-lance architect for short period. Between 1885 and 1899 made sketching tours to Waterford, Conn.; along the Delaware River; to Philadelphia and suburbs; Washington, D. C.; Fort Johnson, Va.; Cleveland, Detroit, Chicago, Milwaukee; along Lake Michigan; St. Paul, Minneapolis; and the Mississippi Basin. Painted earliest watercolors summer of 1888 at White Lake, Sullivan County, N. Y. Spent summer of 1897 sketching on Jersey west shore and in Central Park.

1899-1911

1899-1901 studied under Thomas P. Anshutz and Hugh Breckenridge at the Pennsylvania Academy of the Fine Arts in Philadelphia. 1900 won prize for "original" sketches. 1901-1903 studied under Frank Vincent Dumond at the Art Students' League in New York City. Summer of 1905 went abroad. Made Paris headquarters. 1906 trip to Amsterdam and Belgian coast. 1907 trip to Venice (six weeks), Rome (two days), Florence (two days), and Genoa (overnight). 1908 trip to London, Amsterdam, Bruges, Antwerp, and Brussels. One painting, *The Mills of Meaux*, of 1906 purchased for the Luxembourg. Work included in *Salon d'Automne* of 1908. Exhibited oil paintings in *Salon des Independants* of 1909. Arthur B. Carles introduced Marin to Edward J. Steichen who arranged for the first show of his work at Alfred Stieglitz's Photo-Secession Gallery. In June, 1909, Stieglitz met Marin for the first time. It was at Marin's studio in Paris. December, 1909, returned to America to see the Photo-Secession. Remained there until spring of 1910. Worked on Penobscot Bay, Peconic Bay, and Hudson River subject matter. Returned to Paris. Ten watercolors included in *Salon d'Automne* of 1910. Spent six weeks at Kufstein in the Austrian Tyrol and visited Strasbourg and Nüremberg. Summer of 1911 returned to America. Has never left it since.

1912-1936

Summer of 1912 in Berkshires and Adirondacks. Married December 12, 1912. Work included in Armory Show of 1913. Summers from 1913 to 1936 spent as follows: 1913 at Castorland, N. Y.; 1914 at West Point, Me.; 1915 at Small Point, Me.; 1916 at Echo Lake, Pa.; 1917 at Small Point, Me.; 1918 at Rowe, Mass.; 1919 at Stonington, Deer Isle, Me., and Small Point, Me.; 1920-1924 at Stonington, Me.; 1925 at home, Cliffside, N. J.; 1926 at Chocorua, N. H., Stonington, Me., and Small Point, Me.; 1927 in White Mountains (Franconia Notch, Echo Lake, and Chocorua), on Lake Champlain, and Small Point, Me.; 1928 at Small Point, Me., Stonington, Me., and Lake George; 1929-1930 at Taos and Santa Fe, N. M.; 1931 at Small Point, Me.; 1933-1936 at Cape Split, Addison, Me. Resident of Cliffside, N. J. since 1916.

E. M. B.

Plate Section

1 *London Omnibus* (1908)

5 *Four O'Clock on the Seine* (1909)

9 *Girl Sewing* (1910)

Tyrol at Kufstein, Tyrol Series, No. 3 (1910)

15 *Woolworth Building, No. 31* (1912)

19 *The Little Boat* (1914)

26 *Marin Island, Maine* (1915)

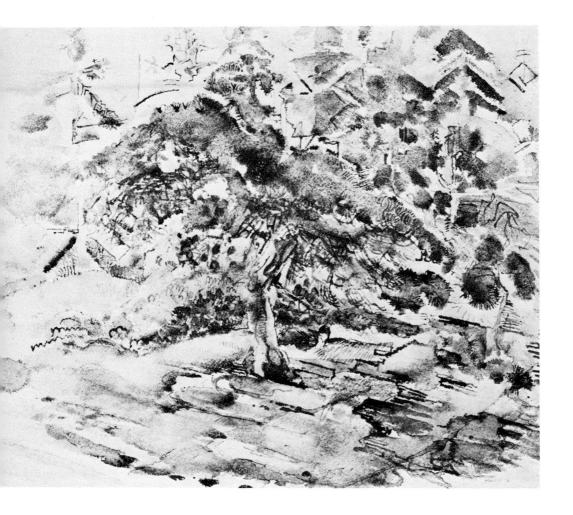

Rock and Scrub Pine, Small Point, Maine (1916)

32 *Tree and Sea, Maine* (1919)

35 *Sunset, Casco Bay* (1919)

39 *Lower Manhattan from the River, No. 2* (1921)

o *Maine Islands* (1922)

53 *Two-master Becalmed, Maine* (1923)

62 *Stonington, Maine* (1923)

68 *The Sun of Suffern* (1925)

78 *Pertaining to Stonington Harbor, Maine* (1926)

84 *Pertaining to Deer Isle—the Harbor. Deer Isle, Maine Series, No. 1 (1927)*

99 *White Mountains, Autumn* (1927)

100 *Street Crossing, New York* (1928)

119 *Broadway, Night* (1929)

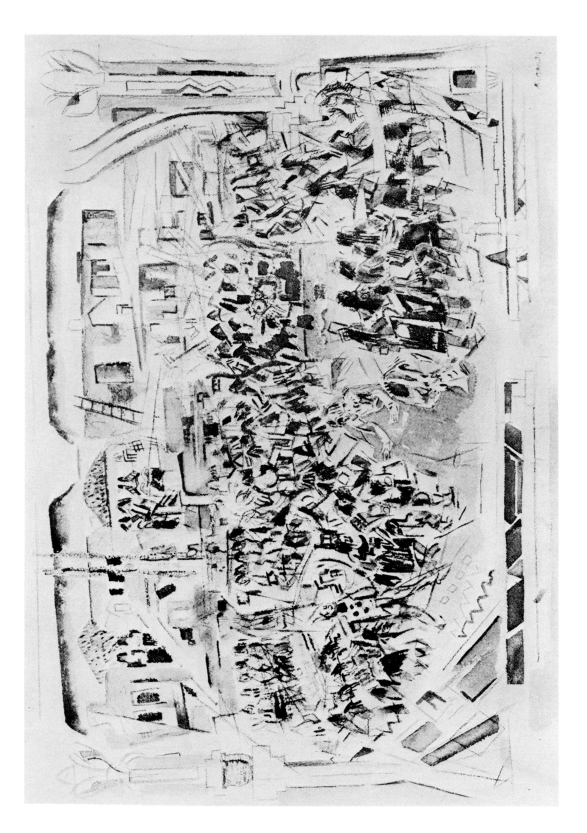

126 *Dance of the San Domingo Indians* (1929)

141 *Deep-sea Trawlers, Maine, No.* 1 (1932)

152 *Tree, No. 1, Cape Split, Maine Coast* (1933)

159 *Young Man of the Sea. Maine Series, No.* 10 (1934)

160 *Lake, Tonk Mountain. Maine Series, No.* 12 (1934)

62 *Rocks and Sea, Small Point, Maine* (1931)

171 *Pertaining to Fifth Avenue and Forty-second Street* (1933)

7 *Women Forms and Sea* (1934)

180 *From Seeing Cape Split* (1935)

Wash Drawing, Study for a Painting (1935). *Actual size*

John Marin, 1915, *at work at* "291"
Photo by Stieglitz

Catalog of the Exhibition

WATERCOLORS

*1 London Omnibus (1908)
    11 x 15 inches

2 Old Houses, Chartres (1908)
    8¼ x 10 inches

3 Mills and Footbridge (1908)
    10½ x 12¼ inches

4 A Rolling Sky, Paris, after Storm (1908)
    12½ x 14 inches

*5 Four o'clock on the Seine (1909)
    14 x 16 inches

6 Along the Seine (1909)
    16¼ x 13¼ inches

7 Movement, Seine, Paris (1909)
    13¼ x 16 inches

8 River Movement, Paris (1909)
    13¼ x 16 inches

*9 Girl Sewing (1910)
    18½ x 15½ inches

10 Mountains and Clouds, Tyrol Series (1910)
    15¼ x 18¼ inches

*11 Tyrol at Kufstein, Tyrol Series, No. 3 (1910)
    15¼ x 18¼ inches

12 Hudson River Palisades (1910)
    15¼ x 18¼ inches

13 Woolworth Building, No. 28 (1912)
    19½ x 16 inches

14 Woolworth Building, No. 29 (1912)
    19½ x 16 inches

*15 Woolworth Building, No. 31 (1912)
    19½ x 16 inches

16 Woolworth Building, No. 32 (1912)
    19½ x 16 inches

17 Broadway, Singer Building (1912)
    19½ x 16 inches

18 Little Tree, Maine (1914)
    13¾ x 15½ inches

*19 The Little Boat (1914)
    16¼ x 19¼ inches

20 Sea, Island, Maine (1914)
    16½ x 19¼ inches

21 Spruce with Moss, Small Point, Maine (1914)
    19½ x 16¼ inches

22 Tree Forms, Autumn (1915)
    19⅛ x 16¼ inches

23 Tree Forms, Maine (1915)
    19¼ x 16¼ inches

24 Rock Shapes and Tree Shapes, Small Point, Maine (1915)
    16 x 19 inches

An asterisk preceding the catalog number indicates that the painting is illustrated by a plate which bears the same number. In the dimensions of the pictures, height precedes width.

25 Pine Trees on Mountain Top, Small Point, Maine (1915)
16⅛ x 19 inches

*26 Marin Island, Maine (1915)
15¾ x 19 inches

27 Sky Forms and Mountain Forms, Delaware Country, Pennsylvania (1916)
16¼ x 19 inches

28 Tree Forms, Delaware Country, Pennsylvania (1916)
14½ x 16¼ inches

*29 Rock and Scrub Pine, Small Point, Maine (1916)
16¼ x 19¼ inches

30 *No title (never exhibited)* (1917)
14 x 16½ inches

31 Tree (1917)
19¼ x 16 inches

*32 Tree and Sea, Maine (1919)
16¾ x 13¾ inches

33 Tree Forms, Stonington, Maine (1919)
16¾ x 13½ inches

34 The Little Boat, Sea and Wind (1919)
16½ x 19¼ inches

*35 Sunset, Casco Bay (1919)
16 x 19½ inches

36 Sun Spots (1920)
16½ x 19½ inches

37 Lower Manhattan (1920)
21 x 26¼ inches

38 Lower Manhattan from the River, No. 1 (1921)
21½ x 26½ inches

*39 Lower Manhattan from the River, No. 2 (1921)
22 x 27 inches

40 Singer Building (1921)
26¾ x 21¾ inches

41 Boat, Deer Isle Thoroughfare (1921)
16¼ x 19¼ inches

42 Deer Isle Thoroughfare (1921)
13½ x 17 inches

43 Movement, the Blue Sea (1921)
16⅜ x 19½ inches

44 Blue-framed Sailboat (1921)
14 x 17⅜ inches

45 Nova-Scotian, No. 15 (1922)
17¼ x 19¾ inches

46 The Red Sun—Brooklyn Bridge (1922)
21¼ x 26 inches

47 Lower Manhattan (composing derived from top of Woolworth) (1922)
21½ x 26¾ inches

48 Camden, across the Bay (1922)
17¼ x 20¼ inches

49 Lobster Smack (1922)
17⅜ x 20¼ inches

*50 Maine Islands (1922)
16¾ x 20 inches

51 The Old Salt (1922)
17 x 19¾ inches

52 Off York Island, Maine (1922)
17¼ x 20¼ inches

*53 Two-master Becalmed, Maine (1923)
16½ x 19½ inches

70

54 Roadside in Maine (1923)
12¾ x 15¼ inches

55 Bare Poles, Two-master, Maine (1923)
15 x 15½ inches

56 Ship, Sea and Sky Forms (1923)

57 Island, Sun and Ships (1923)
16¾ x 19¾ inches

58 Three-master (1923)

59 Schooner off Deer Isle (1923)
16⅞ x 20⅜ inches

*60 Headed for Boston (1923)
17½ x 20¼ inches
Illustrated by color plate—opposite p. 12

61 Before the Wind, Stonington, Maine
(1923)
13¼ x 16¾ inches

*62 Stonington, Maine (1923)
18⅜ x 21⅞ inches

63 Grey Sea (1924)
16½ x 20½ inches

64 Tree Nursery, Closter, New Jersey
(1924)
15½ x 19 inches

65 Palisades Series, No. 4 (1925)
15½ x 19½ inches

66 Eastern Boulevard, Weehawken (1925)
20⅝ x 16¾ inches

67 New York (1925)
20¾ x 17¼ inches

*68 The Sun of Suffern (1925)
17½ x 21⅝ inches

69 Back of Bear Mountain (1925)
17 x 20 inches

70 Mount Hook, Haverstraw, Hudson River
(1925)
15½ x 18¾ inches

71 Movement Related to Downtown New
York (1926)

72 Movement No. 1, Related to Downtown
New York (1926)
17½ x 22¼ inches

*73 Movement No. 2, Related to Downtown
New York (The Black Sun) (1926)
22 x 27 inches
Illustrated by color plate—opposite p. 16

74 Mount Chocorua (1926)
16¾ x 21¾ inches

75 Mount Chocorua. White Mountain Series,
No. 7 (1926)
14¾ x 20 inches

76 Marin Isle. Small Point, Maine Series,
No. 2 (1926)
17½ x 21¾ inches

77 The Pine Tree, Small Point, Maine
(1926)
16¾ x 21¾ inches

*78 Pertaining to Stonington Harbor, Maine
(1926)
16 x 22 inches

79 Movement, Stonington Harbor, Maine
(1926)
13¼ x 19¾ inches

80 Pertaining to Stonington Harbor, Maine,
No. 4 (1926)
16 x 22 inches

81 Movement No. 8, Boat off Deer Isle,
Maine (1926)
16 x 22 inches

71

82 White Horses, Sea Movement off Deer Isle, Maine (1926)
15½ x 20 inches

83 Island Light, off Deer Isle, Maine (1926)
15½ x 20¾ inches

*84 Pertaining to Deer Isle — the Harbor. Deer Isle, Maine Series, No. 1 (1927)
16¾ x 22¼ inches

85 Movement, Sea and Pertaining Thereto. Deer Isle, Maine (1927)
16¾ x 22¼ inches

86 Movement, Boats and Sea. Deer Isle, Maine Series (1927)
13¾ x 18 inches

87 Boats and Sea. Deer Isle, Maine Series, No. 5 (1927)
12⅞ x 16¼ inches

88 Movement, Boat and Sea. Deer Isle, Maine Series, No. 9 (1927)
17½ x 22 inches

89 The Sea and Pertaining Thereto. Deer Isle, Maine Series, No. 15 (1927)
14 x 17¾ inches

90 Movement, the Sea and Pertaining Thereto. Deer Isle, Maine Series, No. 23 (1927)
17 x 21 inches

91 Pertaining to Deer Isle. Deer Isle, Maine Series, No. 24 (1927)
14½ x 17¾ inches

92 Pertaining to Deer Isle — the Harbor. Deer Isle, Maine Series, No. 27 (1927)
18⅛ x 22 inches

93 Pertaining to Deer Isle — the Harbor, No. 2. Deer Isle, Maine Series, No. 28 (1927)
17 x 21¾ inches

94 The Sea and Pertaining Thereto. Deer Isle, Maine Series (1927)
15 x 20 inches

95 Franconia Range, Mountain Peaks (1927)
16¾ x 22⅜ inches

96 White Mountain Country, Summer. Franconia Range, Echo Lake (1927)
17¼ x 22 inches

97 White Mountain Country, Franconia Range. Franconia Notch and Echo Lake, No. 2 (1927)
19¼ x 24 inches

98 White Mountain Country, No. 33. Franconia Notch, Rain and Mist (1927)
15 x 19½ inches

*99 White Mountains, Autumn (1927)
19¼ x 24 inches

*100 Street Crossing, New York (1928)
26¼ x 21¾ inches

101 Midtown New York (1928)
27 x 21¼ inches

102 A Southwester (1928)
17¼ x 22½ inches

103 Schooner Tacks, Deer Isle, Maine (1928)
16⅝ x 22 inches

104 Schooner, Deer Isle, Maine, and Vicinity. Deer Isle, Maine Series, No. 23 (1928)
16¾ x 21¾ inches

105 Boat Fantasy. Deer Isle, Maine Series, No. 30 (1928)
16¾ x 21½ inches

106 From Deer Isle. Deer Isle, Maine Series (1928)
17 x 22 inches

107 Popham Beach. Small Point, Maine Series, No. 1 (1928)
16¾ x 22¼ inches

108 Parker Head. Small Point, Maine Series, No. 4 (1928)
17 x 21½ inches

109 On Morse Mountain. Small Point, Maine Series, No. 6 (1928)
16¾ x 22 inches

110 Sun and Grey Sea. Small Point, Maine Series, No. 16 (1928)
14½ x 16¾ inches

111 Sea Piece. Small Point, Maine Series, No. 19 (1928)
14¾ x 19 inches

112 Sea Piece. Small Point, Maine Series, No. 21 (1928)
14 x 17¾ inches

113 Marin Island. Small Point, Maine Series (1928)
17¼ x 21¾ inches

114 Blue Sea. Small Point, Maine (1928)
14 x 18¼ inches

115 Small Point, Maine, and Vicinity (1928)
16¼ x 21¼ inches

116 Morse Mountain, Small Point, Maine (1928)
16⅞ x 22½ inches

*117 On Morse Mountain, Small Point, Maine (1928)
21 x 16½ inches
Illustrated by color plate—opposite p. 22

118 Schooners (1929)

*119 Broadway, Night (1929)
21⅜ x 26½ inches

120 West Forty-second Street from Ferryboat (1929)
21½ x 26 inches

121 Taos, New Mexico, and Vicinity, No. 1 (1929)
14 x 20 inches

122 Taos, New Mexico, and Vicinity, No. 2 (1929)
14 x 20 inches

123 Red River Country, New Mexico, No. 1 (1929)
21¾ x 30¾ inches

124 Blue Mountain on the Circle Drive near Taos. Red River Country, New Mexico, No. 2 (1929)
21¾ x 30¼ inches

125 Taos Mountain, Pueblo and Mesa (1929)
21¾ x 28¾ inches

*126 Dance of the San Domingo Indians (1929)
22 x 30¾ inches

127 Dance of the Pueblo Indians (1929)
21½ x 28⅜ inches

128 Mountain Forms, New Mexico (1930)
13¾ x 18 inches

129 Valley of the Hondo, New Mexico (1930)
15¼ x 20¼ inches

130 Mountains (Sangre de Cristo), New Mexico (1930)
15½ x 20¼ inches

131 Storm, Taos Mountain, New Mexico (1930)
16⅞ x 21¾ inches

132 Mountain Patterns, New Mexico (1930)
15⅝ x 20⅞ inches

73

133 Near Taos, New Mexico (1930)
15⅛ x 20¼ inches

*134 Storm over Taos, New Mexico (1930)
15¼ x 21 inches
Illustrated by color plate—frontispiece

135 Buoy, Maine (1931)
14¾ x 19¼ inches

136 Wet Weather (1931)
16¾ x 22 inches

137 Tide Riff, Mouth of Kennebec, Maine, Old Fort at Popham in Distance (1931)
16⅛ x 21½ inches

138 Lake Champlain, No. 1 (1931)
16 x 21½ inches

139 Speed, Lake Champlain (1931)
15¾ x 20⅝ inches

140 Boats, Sky and Sea, Small Point, Maine (1932)
15½ x 20¾ inches

*141 Deep-sea Trawlers, Maine, No. 1 (1932)
15½ x 21¾ inches

142 Deep-sea Trawlers, Maine, No. 2 (1932)
15⅛ x 21⅜ inches

*143 Phippsburg, Maine (1932)
15¼ x 19½ inches
Illustrated by color plate—opposite p. 26

144 Rocks, Sea and Boat, Small Point, Maine (1932)
15½ x 20¾ inches

145 Off Bald Head, Small Point, Maine (1932)
15½ x 20½ inches

146 The Coast at the Neck, Maine Coast (1933)
15¼ x 21 inches

147 Four-master off the Cape, Maine Coast (1933)
15½ x 21½ inches

148 Off Flint Island, Maine Coast (1933)
15½ x 22 inches

149 Headland, Cape Split, Maine Coast (1933)
15½ x 20¾ inches

150 Quoddy Head, Maine Coast (1933)
15½ x 22 inches

151 Off Norton Island, Maine Coast (1933)
15¼ x 21½ inches

*152 Tree, No. 1, Cape Split, Maine Coast (1933)

153 Island—Ship's Stern. Maine Series, No. 1 (1934)
16⅞ x 22 inches

154 Boat, Sea and Land. Maine Series, No. 2 (1934)
15½ x 20⅜ inches

155 Headland and Sea. Maine Series, No. 3 (1934)
15½ x 20⅜ inches

156 Wave and Rock. Maine Series, No. 6 (1934)
15¼ x 21½ inches

157 Island—the Ladle. Maine Series, No. 7 (1934)
15¾ x 20½ inches

158 Dead Trees and Sea. Maine Series, No. 9 (1934)
15⅛ x 20 inches

*159 Young Man of the Sea. Maine Series, No. 10 (1934)
15½ x 20½ inches

*160 Lake, Tonk Mountain. Maine Series, No. 12 (1934)
15½ x 20⅝ inches

OILS

161 Jones Beach (1931)
14 x 18 inches

*162 Rocks and Sea, Small Point, Maine
(1931)
22 x 28 inches

163 Rocks and Sea (1932)
21 x 27 inches

164 Mid-Manhattan, I (1932)
28 x 22 inches

165 Mid-Manhattan, II (1932)
28 x 22 inches

166 Looking up Fifth Avenue from Thirtieth
Street (1932)
27 x 22 inches

167 Bryant Square, New York (1932)
21½ x 26½ inches

168 Old Dutch Farmhouse, Tappan, New
York (1932)
22 x 28 inches

169 The Sea, I (1932)
14 x 20 inches

170 The Sea, II (1932)
14 x 20½ inches

*171 Pertaining to Fifth Avenue and Forty-
second Street (1933)
28 x 36 inches

172 Composition, I, Cape Split, Maine
(1933)
22 x 28 inches

173 Composition, II, Cape Split, Maine
(1933)
22 x 28 inches

174 Composition, III, Cape Split, Maine
(1933)
22 x 28 inches

175 Off Cape Split, Maine, I (1934)
22 x 28 inches

176 Off Cape Split, Maine, II (1934)
22 x 28 inches

*177 Women Forms and Sea (1934)
22 x 28 inches

*178 Circus Forms (1934)
28½ x 35¾ inches
Illustrated by color plate—opposite p. 32

179 Study, New York (1934)
22 x 28 inches

*180 From Seeing Cape Split (1935)
23 x 29½ inches

181 Figures, Street Movement (1935)
22 x 28 inches

Check-list of etchings by John Marin

COMPILED BY E. M. BENSON

"It is the business of the cataloguer to describe, not to comment."
WHISTLER

1 PARIS (1905)
Size: height, $4\frac{1}{2}$ inches; width, $7\frac{1}{2}$ inches
Edition: single print
Remarks: plate unsigned and undated; hansom cab and bench in foreground, trees and buildings in background

2 THE SEINE, PARIS (1905)
Size: height, $4\frac{3}{4}$ inches; width, $6\frac{3}{8}$ inches
Edition: three or four prints
Remarks: plate signed and dated "Marin 05" at left center

Included in present exhibition

3 BARGES, SEINE (1905)
Size: height, $5\frac{3}{16}$ inches; width, $6\frac{3}{4}$ inches
Edition: single print
Remarks: plate unsigned and undated; bridge cuts through center of print, building at right, large barge left foreground

Included in present exhibition

4 BRIDGES ACROSS THE SEINE (1905)
Size: height, $5\frac{1}{16}$ inches; width, 7 inches
Edition: single print
Remarks: plate signed and dated "Marin 05" at lower right; bridge in foreground forms enclosure-frame

5 STREET SCENE, PARIS (1905)
Size: height, $7\frac{7}{8}$ inches; width, $5\frac{1}{2}$ inches
Edition: single print
Remarks: plate unsigned and undated; impression of same plate canceled on reverse; stone wall cuts through middleground, roof tops and chimneys in background

6 THE QUAY, SEINE, PARIS (1905)
Size: height, $4\frac{1}{2}$ inches; width, $5\frac{1}{8}$ inches
Edition: single print
Remarks: plate unsigned and undated; two fishermen in foreground, bridge-walk and pedestrians above

The majority of Marin's early prints were never placed on the market. At the time when they were made Marin was inclined to regard them as failures: that is to say, they failed to interest Roullier of Chicago and Katz of New York who were his print dealers from 1906 to 1911. Consequently, Marin saw no reason, at the time, for pulling more than two or three proofs of each so-called failure. The plates for most of these early prints, as well as for those that were published, have either been destroyed or lost. All but two of Marin's prints are straight etchings on copper—the two being line engravings (Nos. 118, 123). From 1905 to 1932 Marin has used four kinds of paper: (1905-1912) mainly Japan and occasionally old Dutch or Fabriano; (1913-1932) Watmann almost exclusively. E. M. B.

2 *The Seine, Paris* (1905)

9 *Bridge Canal, Amsterdam* (1906)

7 PONT-NEUF, PARIS (1905)
Size: height, 7⅞ inches; width, 5$\frac{7}{16}$ inches
Edition: two or three prints
Remarks: plate signed and dated "Marin 05" at lower left; barge emerging from bridge tunnel

8 THE SEINE AT THE LOUVRE (1905)
Size: height, 5 inches; width, 7$\frac{1}{16}$
Edition: single print
Remarks: plate signed and dated indistinctly "Marin 05" at lower right

9 BRIDGE CANAL, AMSTERDAM (1906)
Size: height, 5$\frac{15}{16}$ inches; width, 7½ inches
Edition: about thirty prints
Remarks: plate signed and dated "Marin 06" at lower right; the prints differ only in quality of tone, some having been rubbed in rather heavily, others hardly at all

Included in present exhibition

10 CANAL, AMSTERDAM (1906)
Size: height, 7⅛ inches; width, 5⅛ inches
Edition: about thirty prints
Remarks: plate signed and dated "Marin 06" at lower right

11 AMSTERDAM (1906)
Size: height, 5$\frac{9}{16}$ inches; width, 7⅞ inches
Edition: two or three prints
Remarks: plate signed and dated "Marin 06" at lower left; boats in foreground, buildings and cathedral spires in background

Included in present exhibition

12–13 AMSTERDAM FROM CANAL (1906)
Two states
Size: height, 9½ inches; width, 7½ inches
Edition: single print of each state
Remarks: first state so lightly bitten that signature and date do not appear in print; second state clearly signed and dated "Marin 06" at lower right; etching lines added throughout, also tone giving effect of night scene as contrasted with evenly diffused daylight of first state

14 L'HÔPITAL AT THE SEINE (1906)
Size: height, 5$\frac{1}{16}$ inches; width, 7$\frac{1}{16}$ inches
Edition: six to twelve prints
Remarks: plate signed and dated indistinctly "Marin 06" at lower left

15 NEAR QUAI D'IVRY, PARIS (1906)
Size: height, 5$\frac{15}{16}$ inches; width, 7⅞ inches
Edition: about thirty prints
Remarks: plate signed and dated "Marin 06" at lower right
Included in present exhibition

16 MOULIN ST. MAURICE, MARNE RIVER (1906)
Size: height, 6¾ inches; width, 8⅞ inches
Edition: about thirty prints
Remarks: plate signed and dated "J Marin 06" at lower left; man fishing from boat in standing position in middle-ground, mill building in background

17 CATHEDRAL, LAON (1906)
Size: height, 8$\frac{11}{16}$ inches; width, 5⅜ inches
Edition: about forty prints
Remarks: plate signed and dated "Marin 06" at lower left

18 CATHEDRAL, LAON (1906)
Size: height, 9 inches; width, 6¾ inches
Edition: two or three prints
Remarks: plate signed and dated "Marin 06" at lower left; figure seated on steps in foreground

19 LAON (1906)
Size: height, 6⅞ inches; width, 8¹⁵⁄₁₆ inches
Edition: two or three prints
Remarks: plate signed and dated "Marin 06" at lower left; cathedral tower emerges behind row of buildings

20–21 STREET SCENE, LAON (1906)
Two states
Size: height, 7⅞ inches; width, 5½ inches
Edition: two or three prints of each state
Remarks: plate signed and dated "Marin 06" at lower right; in second state sky above rooftops darkened with crosshatchings, also small area at right of group in courtyard, etc.

22 CATHEDRAL TOWER, LAON (1906)
Size: height, 9 inches; width, 6¾ inches
Edition: single print
Remarks: plate signed and dated indistinctly "Marin 06" at lower right about two inches from bottom

Included in present exhibition

23 VIEW OF LAON (1906)
Size: height, 5½ inches; width, 7⅞ inches
Edition: single print
Remarks: plate signed and dated "Marin 06" at lower right; broad view of Laon country with cathedral towers in distance; plate lightly bitten

24 CATHEDRAL, LAON (1906)
Size: height, 7⅞ inches; width, 5⅝ inches
Edition: two or three prints
Remarks: plate signed and dated "Marin 06" at lower left; front view of the cathedral

Included in present exhibition

25 OLD HOUSE ON SEINE NEAR PARIS (1906)
Size: height, 7⅞ inches; width, 5⅞ inches
Edition: about fifty prints
Remarks: plate signed and dated "J Marin 06" at lower right

Included in present exhibition

26 RUE MOUFFETARD, PARIS (1906)
Size: height, 9 inches; width, 6¾ inches
Edition: twenty-five to thirty prints
Remarks: plate signed and dated "Marin 06" at lower center

Included in present exhibition

27 BAL BULLIER, PARIS (1906)
Size: height, 5½ inches; width, 7⅞ inches
Edition: about thirty prints
Remarks: plate signed and dated "Marin 06" at lower left; man, dog and lamppost on sidewalk in foreground, figures and buildings in background

28 UP THE SEINE, NO. 1 (1906)
Size: height, 5⅛ inches; width, 7¹⁄₁₆ inches
Edition: single print
Remarks: plate signed and dated "Marin 06" at lower right; skeleton of barge right foreground, stone bridge with omnibus and figures middle-ground

29 UP THE SEINE, NO. 2 (1906)
Size: height, 5⅛ inches; width, 6¾ inches
Edition: single print
Remarks: plate signed and dated "Marin 06" at lower left; shore line and buildings at left, water and lightly etched trees at right

30 SEINE, PARIS (1906)
Size: height, 5½ inches; width, 7$\frac{13}{16}$ inches
Edition: single print
Remarks: plate signed and dated "Marin 06" at lower left; omnibus and pedestrians on bridge-walk in middle-ground

31 PARIS STREET SCENE (1906)
Size: height, 5⅛ inches; width, 7⅛ inches
Edition: single print
Remarks: plate signed and dated "Marin 06" at lower left; paper cut at plate edges

Included in present exhibition

32 CATHEDRAL TOWN, FRANCE (1906)
Size: height, 5⅝ inches; width, 8 inches
Edition: single print
Remarks: plate signed and dated "Marin 06" at lower right; stone bridge at right leads to buildings at left; foliage and water in foreground

33 MILLS OF MEAUX, NO. 1 (1906)
Size: height, 5$\frac{1}{16}$ inches; width, 6$\frac{11}{16}$ inches
Edition: single print
Remarks: plate signed and dated indistinctly "Marin 06" at lower right

34 MILLS OF MEAUX, NO. 2 (1906)
Size: height, 7$\frac{13}{16}$ inches; width, 5½ inches
Edition: single print
Remarks: plate signed and dated "Marin 06" at lower right; close view of mill buildings perched above shallow water on wooden supports

35 STREET SCENE, PARIS (1906)
Size: height, 8$\frac{13}{16}$ inches; width, 6⅝ inches
Edition: single print
Remarks: plate signed and dated "Marin 06" at lower left on wall in foreground; print stained slightly with acid spots

36 SQUARE, PARIS (1906)
Size: height, 5½ inches; width, 7¾ inches
Edition: two prints
Remarks: plate signed and dated "Marin 06" at lower left; both proofs acid-stained
Included in present exhibition

37 STREET SCENE, PARIS (1906)
Size: height, 7 inches; width, 5$\frac{1}{16}$ inches
Edition: single print
Remarks: plate signed and dated "Marin 06" at lower left; lamp-post right foreground behind which stand two figures on sidewalk lightly defined; buildings behind and at left
Included in present exhibition

38 NANTEUIL (1906)
Size: height, 5$\frac{9}{16}$ inches; width, 7⅞ inches
Edition: single print
Remarks: plate signed and dated "Marin 06" at lower right and repeated indistinctly at lower left; covered wagon with three-horse team before row of houses

49 *Ponte Ghetto, Venice* (1907)

39 UNLOADING, THE SEINE, PARIS
(1906)
Size: height, $5\frac{7}{8}$ inches; width, $3\frac{15}{16}$
inches
Edition: single print
Remarks: plate signed and dated "Marin
06" at lower left

40 PARIS FROM THE SEINE (1906)
Size: height, $5\frac{7}{8}$ inches; width, $7\frac{7}{8}$
inches
Edition: single print
Remarks: plate signed and dated "J
Marin 06" at lower right; paper badly
creased at plate edges

41 ST. GERMAIN-DES-PRÉS, PARIS
(1906)
Size: height, 8 inches; width, $5\frac{9}{16}$
inches
Edition: About six prints
Remarks: plate signed and dated "Marin
06" at lower left; roof top in foreground, church tower in background

42 OUTSKIRTS OF PARIS (1906)
Size: height, $5\frac{7}{8}$ inches; width, $7\frac{7}{8}$
inches
Edition: about twelve prints
Remarks: plate signed and dated indis-
tinctly "Marin 06" at lower left; row
of houses in background, one marked
"Hotel Du Garde Chasse"

43 COUR DRAGON, PARIS (1906)
Size: height, $7\frac{7}{8}$ inches; width, $5\frac{1}{2}$
inches
Edition: about twenty-five prints
Remarks: plate signed and dated "Marin
06" at lower left; courtyard in shadow
with figures encircled by buildings
bathed in light

Included in present exhibition

44 GONDOLIERS, VENICE (1907)
Size: height, $5\frac{1}{16}$ inches; width, 7
inches
Edition: about twenty-five prints
Remarks: plate signed and dated "Marin
07" at lower left, and "Les Gondoliers
Venezia" at lower right

Included in present exhibition

45 PONTE PARADISO, VENICE
(1907)
Size: height, $7\frac{1}{16}$ inches; width, $5\frac{1}{16}$
inches
Edition: about twenty-five prints
Remarks: plate signed and dated "Marin
07" at lower left, and "Ponte Paradiso
Venezia" at lower right

46 CÀ D'ORO, VENICE (1907)
Size: height, $7\frac{1}{16}$ inches; width, $9\frac{5}{16}$
inches
Edition: about twenty-five prints
Remarks: plate signed and dated "Marin
07" at lower right, and "Cà d'Oro Venezia" at lower left

Included in present exhibition

47 SANTA MARIA DELLA SALUTE,
VENICE (1907)
Size: height, $5\frac{1}{8}$ inches; width, $7\frac{1}{8}$
inches
Edition: about thirty prints
Remarks: plate signed and dated "Marin
07" at lower right and "Santa Maria
della Salute Venezia" at lower left

Included in present exhibition

48 PALAZZO DARIO, VENICE (1907)
Size: height, $7\frac{7}{8}$ inches; width, $5\frac{1}{2}$
inches
Edition: about thirty prints
Remarks: plate signed and dated "Marin
07" at lower left, and "Palazzo Dario
Venezia" at lower right

49 PONTE GHETTO, VENICE (1907)
Size: height, 9½ inches; width, 7½ inches
Edition: about thirty prints
Remarks: plate signed and dated "Marin 07" at left center, and "Ponte Ghetto Venezia" at lower right

Included in present exhibition

50 ON PONTE S. PANTALEO, VENICE (1907)
Size: height, 7⅞ inches; width, 5½ inches
Edition: about thirty prints
Remarks: plate signed and dated "Marin 07" at lower left and "Sur Ponts S Pantalo Venezia" at lower right

51 SESTIERE DI DORSO DURO, VENICE (1907)
Size: height, 7$\frac{1}{16}$ inches; width, 5⅛ inches
Edition: about thirty prints
Remarks: plate signed and dated "Marin 07" at right center, and "Sestiere di Dorsoduro Venezia" at lower left

52 PONTE DI DONNA ONESTA, VENICE (1907)
Size: height, 7⅛ inches; width, 5$\frac{1}{16}$ inches
Edition: about thirty prints
Remarks: plate signed and dated "Marin 07" at lower left, and "Ponte di Donna Onesta Venezia" at lower right

53 CLOCK TOWER OF STA. MARIA ZOBENIGO, VENICE (1907)
Size: height, 7$\frac{5}{16}$ inches; width, 5½ inches
Edition: about thirty prints
Remarks: plate signed and dated "Marin 07" at lower left, and "Clochette de Sta Maria Zobenigo Venezia" at lower right

54 PORTA MONTE GASI [?] MARCO, VENICE (1907)
Size: height, 9$\frac{1}{16}$ inches; width, 6$\frac{11}{16}$ inches
Edition: about thirty prints
Remarks: plate signed and dated "Marin 07" at lower left, and "Porte Mt. Gasi Marco Venezia" at lower right

Included in present exhibition

55 WINDOW, VENICE (1907)
Size: height, 7 inches; width, 5$\frac{1}{16}$ inches
Edition: six to twelve prints
Remarks: plate signed and dated "Marin 07" lower center, and "La Fenêtre Venezia" at lower left

Included in present exhibition

56 CAMPANILE S. PIETRO, VENICE (1907)
Size: height, 6¾ inches; width, 5$\frac{1}{16}$ inches
Edition: about thirty prints
Remarks: plate signed and dated "Marin 07" at lower left, and "Campanile St. Pietro Venezia" at lower right

57 BRIDGE, VENICE (1907)
Size: height, 5⅛ inches; width, 7$\frac{1}{16}$ inches
Edition: about thirty prints
Remarks: plate signed and dated "Marin 07" at lower left center, and "Le Pont Venezia" at lower right

58 THROUGH THE WINDOW, VENICE (1907)
Size: height, 7⅞ inches; width, 5½ inches
Edition: about thirty prints; large additional issue made from steel-faced plate by the magazine *L'Art Décoratif;*

prints pulled on yellowish paper by L. Fort, Paris, whose signature appears at lower left and the magazine's type signature at lower right

Remarks: plate signed and dated "Marin 07" lower center, and "Par la Fenêtre Venezia" at lower right

Included in present exhibition

59 PIAZZETTA S. MARCO, VENICE (1907)
Size: height, $6\frac{3}{4}$ inches; width, $8\frac{15}{16}$ inches
Edition: about thirty prints
Remarks: plate signed and dated "Marin 07" at lower left center, and "Piazzetta S Marco Venezia" at lower left

60 DELLA FAVA [?], VENICE (1907)
Size: height, $9\frac{5}{16}$ inches; width, $6\frac{7}{8}$ inches
Edition: about thirty prints
Remarks: plate signed and dated "Marin 07" at lower left, and "Della Fava Venezia" at lower right

61 CAMPIELLO S. ROCCO, VENICE (1907)
Size: height, $6\frac{5}{16}$ inches; width, $4\frac{13}{16}$ inches
Edition: about thirty prints
Remarks: plate signed and dated "Marin 07" at lower left along edge of plate, and "Campielle S Rocca Venezia" at lower right

62 S. MARCO, VENICE (1907)
Size: height, $5\frac{7}{16}$ inches; width, $7\frac{13}{16}$ inches
Edition: two or three prints
Remarks: plate signed and dated "Marin 07" at lower right, and "Sta Marco Venezia" at lower left

63 CANAL S. PIETRO, VENICE (1907)
Size: height, $4\frac{7}{8}$ inches; width, $6\frac{3}{8}$ inches
Edition: about thirty prints
Remarks: plate signed and dated "Marin 07" at lower left, and "Canali Sta Pietro Venezia" at lower right

Included in present exhibition

64 RUE MOUFFETARD, PARIS (1907)
Size: height, 9 inches; width, $6\frac{5}{8}$ inches
Edition: two or three prints
Remarks: plate signed and dated "Marin 07" at lower right; many figures in foreground, underbitten side wall of building in middle-ground

65 STREET SCENE, PARIS (1907)
Size: height, $7\frac{1}{8}$ inches; width, $5\frac{1}{8}$ inches
Edition: two or three prints
Remarks: plate signed and dated "Marin 07" at lower left; lamp-post, child, and horse in foreground, buildings in background

Included in present exhibition

66 STREET SCENE, PARIS (1907)
Size: height, $7\frac{1}{16}$ inches; width, $5\frac{1}{8}$ inches
Edition: two or three prints
Remarks: plate signed and dated indistinctly "Marin 07" at lower left; façade of four-story building flooded with light, tall tree at left

67 MEAUX (1907)
Size: height, $5\frac{1}{8}$ inches; width, 7 inches
Edition: single print
Remarks: plate signed and dated "Marin 07" lower left center

65 *Street Scene, Paris* (1907)

68–69 MEAUX CATHEDRAL (1907)
First State
Size: height, 9 inches; width, 6$\frac{11}{16}$ inches
Edition: about twelve prints
Remarks: plate signed and dated "Marin 07" at lower right
Second State
Size: height, 8$\frac{5}{8}$ inches; width, 6$\frac{1}{16}$ inches
Edition: about twelve prints
Remarks: plate signed and dated as above; tone border eliminated; print pulled by "professional;" reproduced in *Gazette des Beaux-Arts* of 1908

70 PLACE ST. JACQUES, PARIS (1907)
Size: height, 5$\frac{1}{8}$ inches; width, 7$\frac{1}{16}$ inches
Edition: about twenty-five prints
Remarks: plate signed and dated indistinctly "Marin 07" at lower left; cart in foreground, houses and trees in background

Included in present exhibition

71 WHITE HOUSES, PARIS (1907)
Size: height, 5$\frac{1}{8}$ inches; width, 7 inches
Edition: six to twelve prints
Remarks: plate signed and dated "Marin 07" at lower left; row of white houses in middle-ground

72 NOTRE DAME, PARIS (1908)
Size: height, 12$\frac{1}{2}$ inches; width, 10$\frac{5}{8}$ inches
Edition: about thirty prints
Remarks: plate signed and dated "Marin 08" at lower right, and "NOTRE DAME PARIS" at lower left. Marin says there were two further states of this etching, but no prints of them are now available

Included in present exhibition

73 L'OPERA, PARIS (1908)
Size: height, 10$\frac{11}{16}$ inches; width, 12$\frac{11}{16}$ inches
Edition: about thirty prints
Remarks: plate signed and dated "Marin 08" at lower left, and "L'OPERA PARIS" at lower right

Included in present exhibition

74 LA MADELEINE, PARIS (1908)
Size: height, 12$\frac{13}{16}$ inches; width, 10$\frac{11}{16}$ inches
Edition: about thirty prints
Remarks: plate signed and dated indistinctly "Marin 08" at lower right, and "LA MADELEINE PARIS," also at lower right

75–76 SAINT-SULPICE, PARIS (1908)
First State
Size: height, 12$\frac{15}{16}$ inches; width, 10$\frac{3}{4}$ inches
Edition: about six prints
Remarks: plate signed and dated "Marin 08" at lower left, and "SAN SULPICE PARIS" at lower right; trees at left in foliage, figures and vehicles in foreground
Second State
Size: same as above
Edition: same as above
Remarks: additions made at lower left; trees at left leafless, offering unobstructed view of building in background

77 ST. GERVAIS, RUE GRENIER SUR L'EAU, PARIS (1909)
Size: height, 9$\frac{13}{16}$ inches; width, 7$\frac{7}{8}$ inches
Edition: about six to twelve prints
Remarks: plate signed and dated "Marin 09" at lower right, and "St. Gervais par Rue Grenier Sur L'eau Paris" at lower left; figures and café street scene in foreground, buildings in background

73 *L'Opéra, Paris* (1908)

78 PIERREFONDS (1909)
Size: height, 7¾ inches; width, 9¾ inches
Edition: two or three prints
Remarks: plate signed and dated "Marin 09" at lower right, and "PIERREFONDS" at lower left

79 CATHEDRAL, ROUEN (1909)
Size: height, 9⅞ inches; width, 7¹³⁄₁₆ inches
Edition: about six prints
Remarks: plate signed and dated "Marin 09" at lower right, and "La Cathedral Rouen" at lower left

80 CLOÎTRE ST. MACLOU, ROUEN (1909)
Size: height, 6⅞ inches; width, 8⁷⁄₁₆ inches
Edition: two or three prints
Remarks: plate signed and dated "MARIN 09" at lower right, and "CLOITRE ST MACLOU ROUEN" at lower left

81–85 CLOÎTRE ST. MACLOU, ROUEN (1909)
Five States
Size: height, 6⅜ inches; width, 8 inches
Edition: two or three prints of each of the first four states and about twenty-five prints of the fifth or final state
Remarks: plate signed and dated "Marin 09" at lower right, and "Cloitre St Maclou Rouen" at lower left; standing figure in foreground and tone areas slightly different in each succeeding state: in the first state the figure is etched in outline; additions are made to the lower portion of the figure in the second state; in the third state the figure is heavily etched and toned; in the fourth state no tone is added to the figure and several small areas are scraped out; the fifth state is approximately the same as the preceding one, several lines having been added to the garment of the figure

No. 85 included in present exhibition

86 RUE DE L'ÉPICERIE, ROUEN (1909)
Size: height, 8½ inches; width, 6⅞ inches
Edition: about four prints
Remarks: plate signed and dated "Marin 09" at lower right, and "Rue de L'Epicerie Rouen" at lower left

Included in present exhibition

87 ST. OUEN, ROUEN (1909)
Size: height, 11⅜ inches; width, 9¹⁄₁₆ inches
Edition: about six prints
Remarks: plate signed and dated "Marin 09" at lower left on façade of building, and "St. Ouen Rouen" at lower center

Included in present exhibition

88 THE QUAY, SEINE, PARIS (1909)
Size: height, 9¾ inches; width, 7¹³⁄₁₆ inches
Edition: about six prints
Remarks: plate signed and dated "Marin 09" at lower right; barge and quay in foreground, bridge in middle-ground, buildings in background

89 OLD HOUSE, RUE DES ARPENTS, ROUEN, NO. 1 (1909)
Size: height, 6⅞ inches; width, 8⅜ inches
Edition: about twenty-five prints
Remarks: plate signed and dated "Marin 09" at lower left, and "Vieille Maison Rue des Arpents Rouen" at lower right

91 *The Cathedral near the Old Market, Rouen* (1909)

90 OLD HOUSE, RUE DES ARPENTS,
ROUEN, NO. 2 (1909)
Size: height, $7\frac{3}{16}$ inches; width, $9\frac{11}{16}$
inches
Edition: about twelve prints
Remarks: plate signed and dated "Marin
09" at lower right, and "Vieille Maison Rue des Arpents Rouen" at lower
left; same subject matter as preceding
print

91 THE CATHEDRAL NEAR THE
OLD MARKET, ROUEN (1909)
Size: height, $9\frac{7}{8}$ inches; width, $7\frac{7}{8}$
inches
Edition: about six prints
Remarks: plate signed and dated "Marin
09" at lower left, and "La Cathedrale
par la Vieux Marché Rouen" at lower
right

Included in present exhibition

92 ALONG PONT ST. MICHEL,
PARIS, No. 1 (1909)
Size: height, $7\frac{7}{8}$ inches; width, $9\frac{3}{4}$
inches
Edition: about six prints
Remarks: plate signed and dated "Marin
09" at lower right, and "Par Pont St
Michel Paris" also at lower right; use of
dark tone in sky

93 ALONG PONT ST. MICHEL,
PARIS, No. 2 (1909)
Size: height, $9\frac{1}{8}$ inches; width, $11\frac{5}{16}$
inches
Edition: about six prints
Remarks: plate signed and dated "Marin
09" at lower right, and "Par Pont St
Michel Paris" at lower left

94 NOTRE DAME SEEN FROM THE
QUAI CELESTINS, PARIS (1909)
Size: height, $7\frac{7}{8}$ inches; width, $9\frac{3}{4}$
inches

Edition: about fifty prints
Remarks: plate signed and dated indistinctly "Marin 09" at lower left and
"Notre Dame Vue du Quai Celestins"
at lower right

Included in present exhibition

95 ALONG THE QUAI DES
ORFÈVRES, PARIS (1909)
Size: height, $7\frac{7}{16}$ inches; width, $8\frac{3}{8}$
inches
Edition: about fifty prints
Remarks: plate signed and dated "Marin
09" at left lower center, and "Par Quai
des Orfevres Paris" at lower left; wo-
man washing dog at waterfront center
foreground; barge on Seine, buildings
beyond

96 CHARTRES CATHEDRAL (1910)
Size: height, $11\frac{1}{4}$ inches; width, 9
inches
Edition: about twenty-five prints
Remarks: plate signed and dated "Marin
10" at lower right, and "Chartres" at
lower left

Included in present exhibition

97 FRAUENKIRCHE, NUREMBERG,
NO. 1 (1910)
Size: height, $9\frac{5}{16}$ inches; width, 7
inches
Edition: about ten prints
Remarks: plate signed and dated "Marin
10" at lower left, and "Frauen Kirche
Nürnberg" at lower right

98 FRAUENKIRCHE, NUREMBERG,
NO. 2 (1910)
Size: height, $7\frac{13}{16}$ inches; width, $9\frac{3}{4}$
inches
Edition: about twenty-five prints
Remarks: plate signed and dated "Marin
10" at lower left, and "Frauen Kirche
Nürnberg" at lower right; less factual,
more abstract version of the two

96 *Chartres Cathedral* (1910)

99 PFLANZBADGASSE, STRAS-
BOURG (1910)
Size: height, $8\frac{3}{16}$ inches; width, $9\frac{5}{16}$
inches
Edition: forty-five to fifty prints
Remarks: plate signed and dated "Marin
10" at lower left, and "Pflanzbadgasse
Strasburg" at lower right

100 BROOKLYN BRIDGE, NO. 3
(1911)
Size: height, 11 inches; width, $8\frac{1}{2}$
inches
Edition: two or three prints
Remarks: plate signed and dated "Marin
11" at right; composition different from
every other Brooklyn Bridge etching

101 BROOKLYN BRIDGE, NO. 4
(1911)
Size: height, $8\frac{7}{8}$ inches; width, $11\frac{3}{8}$
inches
Edition: two or three prints
Remarks: plate signed and dated "Marin
11" at right; bridge in middle-ground,
skyscrapers in background

102 BROOKLYN BRIDGE (1913)
Size: height, 7 inches; width, $8\frac{15}{16}$
inches
Edition: about twenty-five prints; plate
steel-faced and several hundred additional prints issued by *The New Republic; cf.,* No. 119
Remarks: plate signed and dated "Marin
Brooklyn Bridge—13" at lower left;
note Marin's earliest use in etching of
the frame within a frame

Included in present exhibition

103 BROOKLYN BRIDGE (1913)
Size: height, $11\frac{5}{16}$ inches; width, $8\frac{3}{4}$
inches
Edition: about twenty prints
Remarks: plate signed and dated "Marin
13 Brooklyn Bridge" at lower left; stac-

cato, broken line technique similar to
that used in print No. 102
Included in present exhibition

104 BROOKLYN BRIDGE NO. 2
(1913)
Size: height, $10\frac{13}{16}$ inches; width, $8\frac{7}{8}$
inches
Edition: two prints
Remarks: plate signed and dated "B.B.
No. 2 Marin 13" at lower left within
border frame of etching; this print car-
ries the alternate title "Song of the
Bridge;" abstract simplification of bridge
jaws as seen from shore line separated
from bridge by strip of water; staccato,
broken line technique

105 BROOKLYN BRIDGE (1913)
Size: height, $8\frac{11}{16}$ inches; width, $6\frac{5}{8}$
inches
Edition: single print
Remarks: unsigned and undated; reverse composition of print No. 104;
wide border frame eliminated

106 BROOKLYN BRIDGE, NO. 6
(1913)
Size: height, $10\frac{13}{16}$ inches; width, $8\frac{7}{8}$
inches
Edition: about twelve prints
Remarks: plate signed and dated "B. B.
6 Marin 13" at lower left; same composition as print No. 103
Included in present exhibition

107 WOOLWORTH BUILDING, NEW
YORK, NO. 1 (1913)
Size: height $11\frac{7}{8}$ inches; width, $9\frac{7}{8}$
inches
Edition: about six prints
Remarks: plate signed and dated "Woolworth 1 Marin 13" at lower right; this
is the second state of this print, no proof
exists of the first state; dramatic tone
highlights throughout

103 *Brooklyn Bridge* (1913)

108 WOOLWORTH BUILDING, NEW YORK, NO. 2 (1913)
Size: height, 12⅞ inches; width, 10⅜ inches
Edition: about six prints
Remarks: plate signed and dated "Woolworth—Marin 13" at lower right

109 WOOLWORTH BUILDING, NEW YORK, NO. 3 (1913)
Size: height, 12⅞ inches; width, 10$\frac{7}{16}$ inches
Edition: about thirty prints
Remarks: plate signed and dated "Woolworth—Marin 13" at lower right within border-frame of etching

Included in present exhibition

110 WOOLWORTH BUILDING, NEW YORK, NO. 4 (1913)
Size: height, 13 inches; width 10$\frac{7}{16}$ inches
Edition: about ten prints
Remarks: plate signed and dated "Woolworth—Marin 13" at lower left within border-frame of etching; simplified and more abstract treatment of same subject matter as preceding print; crosshatching in sky largely eliminated, sun and rays clearly indicated at left of skyscraper

111 ST. PAUL'S AT BROADWAY, NEW YORK, NO. 4 (1913)
Size: height, 6¾ inches; width, 8⅜ inches
Edition: single print
Remarks: plate signed and dated "Marin 14" at lower right; figure leaning against stone column of building at extreme right, figures in abstract movement in foreground, St. Paul's with spire in middle-ground and larger buildings behind

Included in present exhibition

112 BROOKLYN BRIDGE FROM BROOKLYN (1915)
Size: height, 10¾ inches; width, 12$\frac{13}{16}$ inches
Edition: about twelve prints
Remarks: plate signed and dated "Marin 15" at lower left; wide light tone border-frame

Included in present exhibition

113 GRAIN ELEVATORS, WEEHAWKEN (1915)
Size: height, 9$\frac{1}{16}$ inches; width, 11¼ inches
Edition: two or three prints
Remarks: plate signed and dated "Marin 15" at lower left; shore line with grain elevators at right middle-ground and heavily trafficked river beyond as seen from promontory

114 GRAIN ELEVATOR, WEEHAWKEN (1915)
Size: height, 11$\frac{3}{16}$ inches; width, 9 inches
Edition: about six prints
Remarks: plate signed and dated indistinctly "Marin 15" at lower right; abstraction of condensed aspect of grain elevator and activity about it

115 MOVEMENT NO. 2, GRAIN ELEVATORS, WEEHAWKEN (1916)
Size: height, 8$\frac{15}{16}$ inches; width, 11 inches
Edition: two or three prints
Remarks: plate signed and dated "Marin 16" in reverse at lower right; abstraction; tone added

116 GRAIN ELEVATORS, WEEHAWKEN (1917)
Size: height, 7⅞ inches; width, 9⅝ inches

109 *Woolworth Building* (1913)

Edition: single print
Remarks: plate signed and dated "MARIN 17" at lower center; further simplification of two preceding abstract subjects; simple lines and geometrical shapes to which tone has been added

117 STREET SCENE ABSTRACTION (1917)
Size: height, $7\frac{13}{16}$ inches; width, $9\frac{1}{2}$ inches
Edition: two or three prints
Remarks: plate signed and dated indistinctly "Marin 17" at lower left; abstract forms of buildings and street scene objects; line from top-right of plate descends in curve to within two inches of bottom, other lines cross it at right angles; figure and vehicle in separate foreground enclosures

118 WOOLWORTH BUILDING FROM THE RIVER, line engraving (1917)
Size: height, $11\frac{1}{4}$ inches; width, 9 inches
Edition: about twelve prints
Remarks: plate signed and dated indistinctly "Marin 17" at lower right; the tone rubbings differ with each print

119 DOWNTOWN NEW YORK (1921)
Size: height, 7 inches; width, $8\frac{13}{16}$ inches
Edition: about twenty-five prints; plate steel-faced and several hundred additional prints pulled by *The New Republic*; cf., No. 102
Remarks: plate signed and dated "Marin 21" at lower right

120 NASSAU STREET LOOKING SOUTH (1924)
Size: height, $7\frac{15}{16}$ inches; width, $5\frac{15}{16}$ inches

Edition: three or four prints
Remarks: plate signed and dated "Marin 24" at lower right; male figure crossing street from right to left of print

121 DOWNTOWN NEW YORK (1924)
Size: height, $9\frac{7}{8}$ inches; width, $7\frac{13}{16}$ inches
Edition: two or three prints
Remarks: plate signed and dated "Marin 24" at lower right; note enclosures, fully developed by following year

Included in present exhibition

122 DOWNTOWN NEW YORK (1925)
Size: height, $8\frac{5}{16}$ inches; width, $6\frac{9}{16}$ inches
Edition: about twenty-five prints
Remarks: plate signed and dated "Marin 25" at lower right; group of walking figures in foreground enclosure, building at left

Included in present exhibition

123 DOWNTOWN NEW YORK, line engraving (1925)
Size: height, $9\frac{11}{16}$ inches; width, $7\frac{13}{16}$ inches
Edition: about twenty prints
Remarks: plate signed and dated "Marin 25" at lower right; the tone rubbings differ with each print

124 ST. PAUL'S, NEW YORK (1925)
Size: height, $8\frac{5}{16}$ inches; width, $6\frac{5}{8}$ inches
Edition: about twenty prints
Remarks: plate signed and dated "Marin 25" at lower right on gravestone

125 RIVER MOVEMENT (1925)
Size: height, $7\frac{13}{16}$ inches; width, $9\frac{11}{16}$ inches
Edition: about thirty prints

125 *River Movement* (1925)

131 *Sailboat* (1932)

Remarks: plate signed and dated "Marin 25" at lower right; ferryboat and tug in foreground enclosures, skyscrapers in background

Included in present exhibition

126 ST. PAUL'S, NEW YORK (1930)
Size: height, $9\frac{11}{16}$ inches; width, $6\frac{13}{16}$ inches
Edition: about twenty prints
Remarks: plate signed and dated "Marin 30" at lower right; elevator span crosses picture in foreground, St. Paul's and skyscrapers in background

Included in present exhibition

127 SKYSCRAPERS IN CONSTRUC-
TION, NO. 1 (1930)
Size: height, $9\frac{15}{16}$ inches; width, $6\frac{7}{8}$ inches
Edition: about thirty prints
Remarks: plate signed and dated "Marin 30" at lower right ·

Included in present exhibition

128 SKYSCRAPERS IN CONSTRUC-
TION, NO. 2 (1930)
Size: height, $9\frac{15}{16}$ inches; width, $6\frac{7}{8}$ inches
Edition: single print
Remarks: plate signed and dated indistinctly "Marin 30" at lower right; same composition as preceding print; this print bears the artist's notation "only good print—plate destroyed"

129 LOWER END OF MANHATTAN
FROM THE BRIDGE (1931)
Size: height, $6\frac{7}{8}$ inches; width, $9\frac{9}{16}$ inches
Edition: about twenty-five prints
Remarks: plate signed and dated "Marin 31" at lower right

Included in present exhibition

130 BROOKLYN BRIDGE (1931)
Size: height, $6\frac{15}{16}$ inches; width, $9\frac{5}{8}$ inches
Edition: about twenty-five prints
Remarks: plate signed and dated "Marin 31" at lower right

Included in present exhibition

131 SAILBOAT (1932)
Size: height, $6\frac{7}{8}$ inches; width, $9\frac{1}{4}$ inches
Edition: about thirty prints
Remarks: plate signed and dated "Marin 32" at lower left; plate steel-faced in 1936 and large unsigned issue pulled

Included in present exhibition

132 SAILBOAT (1933)
Size: height, $6\frac{3}{4}$ inches; width, $9\frac{3}{8}$ inches
Edition: three or four prints
Remarks: plate signed and dated "Marin 1933" at lower left; further abstraction of preceding subject; withheld from market, considered unsuccessful by artist

Selected Bibliography

BARKER, VIRGIL
"The Water Colors of John Marin." *The Arts*, Feb. 1924, pages 65-84

"John Marin." *Art and Understanding*, Nov. 1929, pages 106-09

BENSON, E. M.
John Marin: the Man and His Work. Washington, D. C., The American Federation of Arts, 1935

"The American Scene." *The American Magazine of Art*, Feb. 1934, pages 57-58

CAFFIN, C. H.
"Maurers and Marins at the Photo-Secession Gallery." *Camera Work*, July 1909, page 41

CRAVEN, THOMAS
"John Marin." *Shadowland*, Oct. 1921

"John Marin." *The Nation*, Mar. 19, 1924, page 321

EGLINGTON, GUY
"John Marin, Colorist and Painter of Sea Moods." *Arts and Decoration*, Aug. 1924, pages 13-14

FLINT, RALPH
"John Marin." *American Art Portfolios*, New York, Raymond and Raymond, Inc., 1936

FRANK, WALDO
"The American Art of John Marin." *McCall's Magazine*, June 1927

GALLATIN, A. E.
American Water-Colourists. New York, E. P. Dutton, 1922

GOODRICH, LLOYD
"Exhibition of Watercolors, Stieglitz Gallery." *The Arts*, Nov. 1930, pages 120-21

HARTLEY, MARSDEN
Adventures in the Arts. New York, Boni & Liveright, 1921, pages 96-101

HASKELL, ERNEST
"John Marin." *The Arts*, Jan. 1922

HIND, LEWIS
Art and I. London, John Lane, 1921, page 178

JEWELL, E. A.
Americans. New York, Alfred Knopf, 1930, page 34

KOOTZ, S. M.
Modern American Painters. New York, Brewer & Warren, 1930, pages 45-47

MC BRIDE, HENRY
"Modern Art." *The Dial*, Feb. 1929, pages 174-75

MARIN, JOHN
Letters of John Marin; edited and with an introduction by H. J. Seligmann. New York, privately printed for An American Place, 1931. (Contains the article "John Marin on Himself" which first appeared in *Creative Art*, Oct. 1928.)

MEIER-GRAEFE, JULIUS
"A Few Conclusions on American Art." *Vanity Fair*, Nov. 1928

MUMFORD, LEWIS
"Marin and Brancusi." *The New Republic*, Dec. 15, 1926, pages 112-13

PHILLIPS, DUNCAN
A Collection in the Making. New York, E. Weyhe, 1926, page 59

ROSENFELD, PAUL
Port of New York; essays on fourteen American moderns. New York, Harcourt, Brace and Co., 1924, pages 153-66

"Marin Show." *The New Republic*, Feb. 26, 1930, pages 48-50

"Essay on Marin." *The Nation*, Jan. 27, 1932, pages 122-24

SELIGMANN, H. J.
"American Water Colours in Brooklyn." *International Studio*, Dec. 1921, sup. 159-60

STRAND, PAUL
"John Marin." *Art Review*, Jan. 22, 1922

"Marin Not an Escapist." *The New Republic*, July 25, 1928, pages 254-55

See also reviews of exhibitions by E. A. Jewell in *The New York Times*, by Henry McBride in *The Sun*, and by Lewis Mumford in *The New Yorker*.